RSA
TYPEWRITING SKILLS
BOOK ONE

 Heinemann Educational Books
in association with the RSA

Heinemann Educational Books Ltd
22 Bedford Square, London WC1B 3HH

LONDON EDINBURGH MELBOURNE AUCKLAND
HONG KONG SINGAPORE KUALA LUMPUR
NEW DELHI IBADAN NAIROBI JOHANNESBURG
PORTSMOUTH (NH) KINGSTON

First published 1986
Reprinted 1986

British Library Cataloguing in Publication Data
RSA Typewriting skills.
Book 1
1. Typewriting
I. Royal Society of Arts
652.3   Z49
ISBN 0-435-45174-X

Design and typesetting by The Pen and Ink Book Company Ltd, London

Printed in Great Britain by William Clowes Ltd, Beccles and London

Foreword

The RSA is very conscious of the important role its vocational qualifications play for students, teachers, trainers and employers. They provide that vital link by which the worlds of education and employment are joined together. RSA certification of an individual's achievement demonstrates to the employer that a worthwhile and trustworthy standard has been reached, and that standard is one recognised nationally and internationally. In order to maintain those standards and that recognition, the RSA ensures that its certificates are meeting the changing needs of the modern world.

The RSA's new Typewriting Skills syllabuses are designed to prepare people of all ages for the changing environment of working life. The Stage I scheme certifies competence in basic typewriting skill, which is the essential common foundation for further development, whether into more advanced and specialised typewriting functions or into text-processing using new forms of technology. The RSA's scheme has also been developed in such a way that it is fully criterion-referenced so that students, teachers and employers know precisely what is required and what skills the holder of an RSA Stage I Certificate in Typewriting Skills *demonstrated at the time of the examination*. The RSA approach, therefore, concentrates on the demonstration of performance of skills and activities which are applicable and transferable to a wide range of business situations. We want to help students to be aware of the skills that they 'own', and to give them the confidence to use, and indeed develop, those skills in a rapidly changing environment.

The RSA has recognised that teachers and candidates would welcome learning material designed to assist in the achievement of these aims. It therefore decided to help those preparing for the new certificate by producing a book specifically designed to encourage the new approach to Typewriting Skills.

The text has been prepared for the RSA by Margaret Rees-Boughton, Consultant to the RSA in Office Subjects.

This is the first time that the RSA has taken such a step and we hope that students, teachers and employers find it useful.

Martin Cross
Examinations Director
RSA

Contents

Note: Items B1 – B9 and C1 – C12 refer to sections B and C of the RSA Typewriting Skills Stage I syllabus (see pages 3 – 5).

Index

General Introduction

WHO THIS BOOK IS FOR

Those who have mastered the keyboard and are familiar with the basic operations of the machine; and are now preparing for the RSA Stage I exam in Typewriting Skills.

It provides training in the basic knowledge and skills required for occupations based on typewriting, for example, copy-typist, receptionist-typist, clerk-typist, audio-typist, shorthand-typist and word processor operator.

What it assumes

In order to use this book effectively, you must already be able to:

- operate the keyboard, including figures, shift and fractions;
- use all machine parts for:
    adjustments – e.g. paper release, margin set/release, paper guide, paper scale
    alignment – e.g. line-space regulator, variable line-spacer, interliner, return, half-line spacing (for superscripts and subscripts)
    tabulation – setting and cancelling stops, tabulator key or bar;
- use A4 and A5 paper.

What else is assumed

A sound knowledge of English is essential.

In an office a typist is rarely, if ever, required to copy perfect work.

Typewriting skills, therefore, represent much more than keyboarding and the use of machine functions, such as tabulation, backspacing and margin setting. Most original work is handwritten, which varies in style from one writer to another. Typists need to be familiar with words in common use and able to understand meanings of passages, if they are not to have difficulty interpreting scripts. They also depend upon the skill of error-spotting when re-reading their own work – and for this, understanding of meaning is essential.

Accuracy is of major importance for success in the exam; not only must the words typed be the right ones, they must also be copied with the same capital letters and punctuation as in the draft. Any weakness in language skill is bound to affect attainment.

Some knowledge of business practice is expected, but this is restricted to customary uses and procedures of typewriting and stationery. For instance, people in offices rely on the typist to include today's date in all correspondence, unless otherwise instructed; a typist should not need to be told when to use a letterhead; and it would suggest lack of understanding if pre-printed headings on a form (e.g. 'Name' or 'Address') were copied again by a typist.

It is important for two reasons that typists know about such general matters of business practice:

1   Instructions in the exam paper will be given (or not given) on the assumption that candidates will be able to follow business practice.
2   Anyone who has not developed an awareness of stationery used and customary formats for, say, letters may waste time in the examination. They may worry whether to follow the general format used in a draft because they do not recognise it as standard practice.

meaning in a dictionary. If you were able to copy the legible draft without difficulty you should still check the word after the exam so as to imprint new word(s) in your memory for future use.

PAPER A185 6 NOVEMBER 1985

Did you fulfil the following Objectives?

B2   *Confirming facts*

In **Task 1** did you complete the gaps with '*Norway Spruce transplants*'?

B4   *Spelling*

In **Task 1** did you spell in full: Dear (Sirs); your; develop; your reference; catalogue; believe; recommend; should; approximately; should; years?
  In **Task 2** did you spell in full: advertisement; received?
  You should have kept the following abbreviations:
  Task 1 – Ltd; Hants; cm
  Task 2 – etc
  Task 3 – ext
  Task 4 – ext
  Task 6 – cm

Other points to notice:

Task 1

The special mark 'FOR THE ATTENTION OF . . .' is an example of the use of capitals as in the draft (see Objective C5).

Task 3

Leaving space is particularly important. The exact number of spaces must be left for the inset, and clear lines around and between the Pack details. Remember, you can leave an extra few spaces when the instruction says 'at least'.

Task 6

Did you remember to date the form with the exam date (or the date on which you typed the paper)?

The RSA syllabus for Typewriting Skills sets out what you will have to do in the exam to demonstrate competence in typewriting. It highlights the difference between keyboarding and basic 'typewriting skill'.

The three sections

The syllabus groups into three sections (A, B and C) the abilities needed in a typewriting-based job:

A *Rate of production:* the ability to produce work at reasonable speed;
B *Accuracy of content:* ability and willingness to pay meticulous attention to detail;
C *Presentation of work:* a knowledge of general styles and good business practice for use of stationery; plus the patience and care to make work attractive in appearance.

What the certificate means

An RSA Stage I Typewriting Skills certificate means the successful candidate has shown that s/he can type:

1 *at a reasonable speed* – that is, at a rate of production adequate to complete six business tasks including a carbon copy and an envelope within two hours;
2 *accurately* – that is, with at least 98.5% accuracy;
3 work that is *attractive in appearance* – that is, present work effectively and in line with current styles and conventions.

For each of the three sections of the syllabus a clear statement is made of the standard that must be reached to receive a Pass (see 6.3 on page 9). The standard required for the award of Distinction is covered separately (see 6.2 on page 8).

The holder and future users (e.g. employers) of the certificate will therefore understand what must be done, and to what standard, in order to gain a Pass.

It is important to recognise that 'competence' means ability in all aspects of any activity. In typewriting, work that is inaccurate is unusable in an office, no matter how quickly it is produced, or how beautifully it is presented. Equally, it is important that a typist should be able to combine productivity with accuracy and ability to present work in styles that make it intelligible. Therefore, a Pass cannot be awarded unless the standard for *each* section of the syllabus is reached.

The Stage I scheme assesses basic typewriting skills at elementary level, that is, those needed by a typist in a first job, and the exam consists of tasks which are typical of the routine or general work of any office.

The test papers are not always set for the same type of business. It is important that typewriting skill is developed so that it can be used to produce *any document in any context*.

The following syllabus will apply with effect from the 1986 Autumn series of examinations.

Special points checklist for practice exam papers

PAPER 187 13 JUNE 1985

Did you fulfil the following Objectives?

B2   Confirming facts

In **Task 1** did you complete the gap with 'Dear Mr *Timms*'?

B4   Spelling

In **Task 1** did you spell in full: your; and; which; will; opportunity?
   In **Task 3** did you spell in full: July?
   In **Task 5** did you spell in full: received; sufficient; would; approximately?
   You should have kept the following abbreviations:
Task 2 – USA; UK; USSR
Task 3 – am
Task 4 – BC
Task 5 – Inc; USA; no 821B; ft; no 6167E
Task 6 – plc; in

B9   Correcting material containing errors

In **Task 4** did you correct to: built; we; BC; Stonehenge; was; Aubrey; stones?

Other points to notice:

Task 1

Objective C5 instructs that capital letters must be used as shown in the draft. If, however, you wished to add emphasis to the special mark 'Confidential' and underline it, this would not be penalised (see C5 in marking scheme on page 12).

Task 2

It is clear from the draft that the writer prefers a clear space after the asterisk (*) in the footnote, and you should copy this sort of implied instruction and concentrate on accuracy. The marking scheme refers only to consistency in style of presentation, which is inapplicable here as there is only one footnote. Therefore, if you did not leave the space no penalty applies.

Task 3

Use of the dash/hyphen key for 'to' occurs several times. Spacing must be the same throughout (either as 5-9 years *or* 5 – 9 years) – see Objective C3c). Hyphens must be used (no spaces) for FEET-FIRST, dance-theatre and Cheadle-on-Sea.

Task 5

You may have found the words 'jacuzzis', 'sauna' and 'sienna' unfamiliar. If so, and whenever you meet a new word, check the

1 Aims

This scheme defines typewriting competence as a totality of speed, accuracy and presentation skills. Candidates will therefore be assessed in each of these 3 elements and for award of a certificate must meet the criteria specified for all 3 of them.

   The overall aim of the scheme is to test the candidate's ability to meet the typewriting requirements of the discerning employer.

2 Target Population

The beginner typist who has a sound command of English and basic numeracy, and some knowledge of business practice.

   The Stage I scheme tests knowledge and skill at a level suitable as a basis for further development and training, and for employment.

3 Assessment Objectives

Section A – Rate of production

A   Candidates must use their machines to work at a rate of production adequate to complete 6 business tasks within 2 hours.
   Working from handwritten and typewritten drafts within the 6 tasks they must produce:

A1   Letter
A2   Memorandum
A3   Pre-printed form completed with given information
A4   Single carbon copy
A5   Envelope
A6   Notice, advertisement etc
A7   3-column table with single line headings
A8   Continuous text (article, extract, etc)

The production rate at this level takes into account time for: machine manipulation, organisation of time and materials, scanning, reading, interpreting (including use of context to identify words as necessary), use of styles and conventions, checking and correcting, for the purpose of processing drafts in any context.

Section B – Accuracy of content

B   Candidates must use their machines to produce work which after application of appropriate correction techniques/materials, is accurate in context, including compliance with explicit and implicit instructions about content.
   They must:

B1   INSERT date on letters, memos and forms as appropriate
B2   CONFIRM facts, e.g. names, dates, from overt information, without explicit instruction
B3   INCORPORATE amendments to text:
      (a) deletions with replacement
      (b) deletions without replacement
      (c) correction signs:

new paragraph [or //

run on ⌐

insertion ⋀ with word(s) above
   or balloon with arrow

no marginal instructions

THIS FORM - FOR USE IN WORKING TASK 6 - MUST BE INSERTED INSIDE THE COVER
OF YOUR ANSWER BOOK AT THE CONCLUSION OF THE EXAMINATION. IF BOTH SIDES
OF THIS FORM ARE USED ONE ATTEMPT MUST BE CANCELLED.

S T U D I O   P R I N T S   L I M I T E D

67 The Broadway London WC1A 4RT   Telephone: 01-957 2438

ORDER FOR COLOUR PRINTS

NAME AND ADDRESS

PROOF NUMBER	SIZE	NUMBER REQUIRED
....	....	....
....	....	....
....	....	....
....	....	....
....	....	....
....	....	....

SIGNATURE ....

DATE ....

transpose horizontally ⌣ or balloon
    with arrow

transpose vertically ⌡⌠ or balloon
    with arrow   } no marginal instructions

stet .... with ☑ in margin

B4 SPELL the following words accurately from the abbreviations as shown:

accom.	accommodation	rec(s).	receipt(s)
a/c(s).	account(s)	rec.	receive
ack.	acknowledge	recd.	received
advert(s).	advertisement(s)	recom.	recommend
appt(s).	appointment(s)	ref(s).	reference(s)
approx.	approximate/ly	refd.	referred
bel.	believe	resp.	responsible
bus.	business	sec(s).	secretary/ies
cat(s).	catalogue(s)	sep.	separate
cttee(s).	committee(s)	sig(s).	signature(s)
co(s).	company/ies	suff.	sufficient
def.	definite/ly	temp.	temporary
dev.	develop	thro'.	through
ex.	exercise		
exp(s).	expense(s)	sh.	shall
exp.	experience	shd.	should
gov(s).	government(s)	wh.	which
gntee(s).	guarantee(s)	wd.	would
immed.	immediate/ly	w.	with
incon.	inconvenient/ence	wl.	will
mfr(s).	manufacturer(s)	yr(s).	year(s)
misc.	miscellaneous	yr(s).	your(s)
necy.	necessary	dr.	dear
opp(s).	opportunity/ies		

days of the week (e.g. Thurs., Fri.)
months of the year (e.g. Jan., Feb.)
words in address (e.g. Cres., Dr.)
complimentary closes (e.g. ffly.)

(N.B. Full stops with the words shown above indicate abbreviations, not punctuation.)

and RETAIN other commonly used abbreviations such as 'NB', 'etc', 'eg'; '&' in company names, etc ('&' in text to be expanded)

B5 INSERT special marks, e.g. Confidential, Attention line, as instructed

B6 INDICATE enclosure as implied in the draft

B7 SELECT and TRANSFER appropriate details to envelopes

B8 COPY unfamiliar and/or foreign words from legible draft

B9 PRESENT IN CORRECTED FORM material containing:

(a) obvious typographical errors
(b) obvious errors of agreement and punctuation, including apostrophes

These will be indicated in the draft by circling the incorrect word(s) and will be confined to one specified task in typescript

Typist: please complete the order form for mailing today.

The name/address is:

Praxiteles Forestry Group
Praxiteles House
Adam Street
LONDON,
WC2N 6AJ

The following prints are to be ordered:

Proof Number 7A/23 size 7.5 cm x 5 cm 200 copies

15 copies of 7B/91 size 10 cm x 7.5 cm

C   Candidates must use their machines to produce work which, after application of appropriate correction techniques/materials, is effectively presented and in line with current styles and conventions – including compliance with explicit and implicit instructions about presentation.
   They must:

C1   IDENTIFY and USE limited supplies of stationery economically and effectively

C2   PRODUCE clean, uncreased work

C3   USE CONSISTENTLY (throughout a task) a currently accepted style of presentation of:
(a) abbreviations indicating measurements/weights/times/money
(b) words/figures
(c) words/symbols (including dash/hyphen key for 'to')
(d) punctuation (i.e. open or full)
(e) paragraphing (including numbered/lettered paragraphs, sub-paragraphs and listed items)
(f) alternative spellings
(g) fractions
(h) line spacing
(i) leader dots
(j) material in columns

C4   INSET indicated portions of a task as instructed, from left-hand margins

C5   USE spaced capitals, closed capitals, initial capitals and underlining for emphasis in headings and in text, as shown in draft

C6   USE consistently blocked *or* centred style at own discretion

C7   USE specified line spacing

C8   ALLOCATE SPACE of specified size (which may be expressed in terms of measurement or line spacing) e.g. for margins, addresses, illustrations

C9   USE, in the absence of instructions, a left-hand margin and a top margin of at least 13 mm (½″)

C10   LEAVE, in the absence of instructions, a minimum of one clear line space:
(a) between paragraphs
(b) before and after headings
(c) before footnotes
(d) between complimentary close and signatory
(e) before and after separate items within a document, e.g. date, reference

C11   USE correcting materials/techniques as necessary to make inconspicuous corrections

C12   INSERT given information on pre-printed documents;
MAKE DELETIONS effectively

TASK 5

Typist: A5 paper please

PRAXITELES   FORESTRY   GROUP

Spaced caps → Price List

REFERENCE	DESCRIPTION	PRICE (£)
A	50 Trees	80
B	100 Trees	50
C	Game Spinney	260
D	Beech Hedging ~~Shrubs~~	76
E	Game Cover	184
F	Ornamental Trees	300
G	Christmas Trees*	295
H	Hedgerow Shrubs	129
I	Shelter Belt Trees	90
J	Lombardy Poplars	35

* REMEMBER Pack G needs only 1000 m² of land!

(Prices valid November 1985 — October 1986.)

4 Form of Assessment

4.1 Candidates will be assessed in a 2-hour production test set and marked by the RSA and consisting of 6 practical typewriting tasks presented in handwriting and typescript.

4.2 Nature of tasks: the material given will be concerned with topics drawn from the business functions e.g. purchasing, personnel, accounts, that are common to the majority of business, commerce and professional offices.

4.3 The stationery provided for completion of the tasks will be:

A4 letterhead	2
A4 memo	2
A4 plain white	4
A5 plain white	2
A4 yellow flimsy	2
DL manilla envelope	1
Printed form for completion	2

No additional stationery will be allowed.

4.4 Instructions not under Objective B3 will be given in handwriting and circled to distinguish them from the text.

4.5 Candidates may use calculators and English dictionaries in the examination.

4.6 Any form of correcting material or correcting mechanism may be used.

4.7 The RSA does not provide carbon paper, correcting materials, calculators or dictionaries. Candidates are advised to check with their centres well before the examination whether they need to bring any of these.

5 Criteria of Assessment

Marking Scheme*

Note: Obvious machine faults will not be penalised.

A *Production rate* – all tasks (including carbon copy and envelope) to be completed except as provided for in Section B2 'Omissions' below.
B *Accuracy*
A word is defined as including following or associated punctuation and spacing.

A word fault is any word which is not 100% accurate.

Groups of figures count as 1 word (e.g. 125 for 100 = 1 error).

One word fault only will be ascribed to any one word (e.g. 'acommodatoin' counts as only one word fault in spite of several faults in the word, but Presentation faults may be applied in addition (e.g. dates inappropriately aligned against pre-printed heading).

The same fault appearing more than once counts as a word fault each time.

* Subject to confirmation

Typist: please retype correcting the words that are circled.

Type on A4 paper

PRAXITELES FORESTRY GROUP

PLANTING SERVICES OFFERED TO FARMERS

Planting can be designed to provide boundary demarcation,
shelter-belts to improve productivity, stock-proof hedging,
shade and ultimately timber for a variety of uses. Trees
can aslo produce a crop such as Christmas trees or provide
Game Cover to increase an estates sporting value.

In addition tree planting can contribute to wild life
conservation. Also it improves the local enviroment by
enhancing the appearance of the countryside.

In conjunction with our regional nurseries Praxiteles
Forestry Group can offer a full planting service for small
woodlands.

The fully-qualified foresters is available to carry out all
aspects of plantation establishment, eg draining, fencing,
planting and subsequent maintenance. Where necessary the
clearing of scrub can be undertaken as well. All our staff
apprecate the importance of small woodland areas to the
farmer.

For information about the tree planting services availalbe
to farmers, please contact Susan Ferris or Christopher Jones
on 01-839 1691 ext 45.

SF/CJ

There are two main types of word fault:

1 words which contain typing/spelling/punctuation faults
2 whole words which are omitted or added.

(N.B. Carbon copies and envelopes will be treated in the same way as all other pieces of work and will be marked in the usual way, *except* in the case of carbon copies where word faults already penalised on the top copy/original will not be penalised again.)

1 *Typing/spelling/punctuation faults*
These are words which

1.1 contain an incorrect character, whether from mis-spelling, mis-typing, incorrect alignment of character (including irregular left-hand margin) or any other cause (e.g. handwritten character – except accents, etc.).

1.2 have omitted or additional characters or spaces within the word (including omissions caused by faulty use of correction materials/techniques, e.g. hole in paper or character left illegible by correcting material).

1.3 have more than 2 spaces following them, unless these words have already been penalised.

1.4 contain overtyping, including overtyping of pre-printed material (per line of entry) in letters, memos and forms. (Satisfactory stretching or squeezing of words without overlapping will not be penalised.)

1.5 do not contain initial capitals which are shown in draft, or contain initial capitals which are not shown in draft.

2 *Omissions and additions*
A word fault in this category is defined as

2.1 each word which should be in the text, but has been omitted

2.2 each word which should not be in the text but has been added, or not removed.

2.3 any instruction to transpose not carried out, regardless of the amount of material involved.

C *Presentation faults*
A presentation fault means any instance of failure to comply with the Objectives:

C1 incorrect stationery used

C2 task dirty (e.g. thumb marks), creased or torn
(N.B. It is not necessary to fold or tear A4 memo paper but if this is done cleanly and effectively no penalty will be incurred.)

C3 Inconsistency throughout a task of a currently accepted form of presentation of:

(a) abbreviations indicating measurements/weights/times/money
(b) words/figures
(c) words/symbols (including dash/hyphen key for 'to') ampersand to be retained, e.g. in company names, and expanded in text
(d) punctuation (at least one space required after punctuation mark)
(e) paragraphing (including numbered/lettered paragraphs, sub-paragraphs and listed items)
(f) alternative spellings
(g) fractions
(h) line spacing
(i) leader dots

TASK 3

Heading in closed caps

Typist: A4 paper please

P R A X I T E L E S   FORESTRY   GROUP

INFORMATION   FOR   PACK A   AND   PACK B

These packs can consist of the following young trees:

Inset 10 spaces

Ash	Beech
Field Maple	Horse Chestnut
Lime	Norway Maple
Silver Birch	Sycamore
White Poplar	White Willow

The Buyer can choose in ~~lots~~ multiples of 10 any of the trees listed above and order in lots of 50 or 100.

Typist: please leave 4 clear lines where indicated by arrows

Typist: please leave a space at least 7.5 cm (3 in) wide.

Pack A (50 Trees) – £50

Pack B (100 Trees) – £80

However, if you need larger quantities of specific trees please ask for a special quotation. // All trees are supplied with plastic spiral guards to protect them against ~~animal~~ damage.

For more information please contact Susan Ferris or Christopher Jones on 01-839 1691 ext 45

or write to:

Praxiteles Forestry Group
Praxiteles House
Adam Street
LONDON
WC2N 6AJ

(j) material in columns. Whole *figures* may be ranged to the left or the right of a column; *words* may be ranged to the left, blocked or centred

C4 Indicated portions of a task not inset from left-hand margin as instructed

C5 Spaced capitals/closed capitals/initial capitals/underlining for emphasis in headings and in text not as shown in the draft. (N.B. Unrequested underlining of headings will not be penalised. Consistent incorrect use of capitals/underlining in related headings within a task will incur 1 fault only.)

C6 Blocked or centred style (at own discretion) not used consistently for the same type of item throughout a task (e.g. paragraphs in one style with headings in another style is not a fault). Centred style headings and/or material in notices/advertisements not technically accurate to within 13 mm (½″) horizontally. (N.B. 1 fault only if all examples are consistent with a major item centred inaccurately.)

C7 Specified line spacing incorrect

C8 Allocation of space of specified size not correct

C9 Top margin less than 13 mm (½″) } either or both margins
     Left margin less than 13 mm (½″)

C10 Each task instancing *no* clear line space

     (a) consistently between paragraphs
     (b) before and after headings
     (c) before footnotes
     (d) for signature on letters
     (e) before and after separate items within a document
     in the absence of instructions

C11 Each word instancing unsightly and conspicuous correction that results in:

     (a) characters appearing blurred or bold in contrast with uncorrected work
     (b) smoothness of paper being impaired
     (c) substantial mis-alignment of character(s) i.e. half-linespace or more
     (d) hole in paper unless already penalised under B12 as a word fault

     (N.B. White correcting fluid on coloured stationery will not be penalised.)

C12 Information inappropriately inserted on pre-printed documents (e.g. more than one line space above or below).

6 Criteria for certification*

6.1 Results will be graded Distinction, Pass or Fail.

* Subject to confirmation.

TASK 2

(Memo)

From   Sales Manager

To   All Regional Representatives

Ref   CJ/244

Last month's advert. which was (featured prominently) in "Farm Seasons" seems to have been very successful. We have certainly recd. a number of enquiries and, as you know, we are forwarding these to you. Please will you organise visits to the sites in question as soon as possible so that this initial enthusiasm is not lost!

Several organisations have written to us to ask if we could send a speaker to one of their evening meetings to talk about the importance of trees, etc, in the countryside.

If you would be willing to undertake such assignments please will you contact me so that I can pass the information to the various organisations concerned.

149

6.2 For award of a Stage I Certificate with Distinction candidates must fulfil Objective A by working at a production rate of 450 words per hour (i.e. completing all the 6 tasks); Objective B with no more than 5 word faults; *and* Objective C with no more than 5 presentation faults.

6.3 For award of a Stage I Pass Certificate candidates must fulfil Objective A by working at a production rate of 450 words per hour (i.e. completing all the 6 tasks); Objective B with no more than 14 word faults; *and* Objective C with no more than 9 presentation faults.

6.4 The results slip issued to all candidates will indicate the grade awarded on each of the three elements of the assessment.

7 Notes

7.1 Reading time: unlike the previous Typewriting examinations, where reading time was taken as an additional 10 minutes, this scheme incorporates that 10 minutes within the increased overall two hours allowed.

7.2 Warm-up material: the examination paper will not include any 'warm-up' material. At the discretion of the Local Secretary, such material may be provided locally for practice before the start of the examination.

TASK 1

Typist: carbon copy and envelope please

Our ref CJ/137

FOR THE ATTENTION OF MR A K THOMPSON

Fairacre Farms Ltd

Monxton

ANDOVER

Hants SP11 8DP

Dr. Sirs

Thank you for yr. letter received today in response to our advertisement in last month's issue of "Farm Seasons".

Obviously we are pleased that you wish to ~~further~~ dev. two acres of woodland. For yr. ref. we enclose a copy of our cat., which contains some ~~interesting~~ valuable information about the different packs we have available. // We bel. that Pack C (Game Spinney) and Pack E (Game Cover) may prove to be the most suitable and we can recom. these to you.

May we suggest that groups of similar ~~species~~ shd. be planted together in approx. 120 cm centres.

In addition we also / supply Christmas Tree Packs comprising Norway Spruce transplants between 20 cm ~~~~ and 50 cm in height. These shd. be ready for sale within four yrs., although this is dependent upon growing conditions. Only about a quarter of an acre is ~~required~~ for Pack G, which consists of 2,500 N__ S__ t__.

Our regional representative will be pleased to call to see you in order to view the proposed site. We look forward to hearing from you soon.

Yours ~~ad~~ faithfully
PRAXITELES FORESTRY GROUP

C Jones
Sales Manager

Developing Accuracy

Introduction

Section B of the Stage I RSA Typewriting Skills syllabus requires that 'candidates must use their machines to produce work which, after application of appropriate correction techniques/materials, is accurate in content, including compliance with explicit and implicit instructions about content'.They must fulfil the objectives with no more than fourteen word faults.

This section also lists the items that will appear in every Stage I exam (see B1 – B9 on pages 3 – 4). Most of these are activities that can be applied to *any* document – and will be transferable to any office job based on typewriting.

The practice material included in Part One of this book covers the sort of work that you will have to do when typing business documents for individuals rather than companies; and is typed on plain paper. *Some of the practice items included here will be more difficult than the ones you will be expected to do in the exam tasks.*

Each chapter contains a section 'In the exam' to give you some guidance and there are specimen tasks in Part Three for straightforward copy-typing to develop your accuracy (see pages 118 –21). You should use these to help you prepare for the exam, and if you are able to complete all of the practice material without difficulty, you will be confident of being able to cope with the exam tasks.

Practice materials are provided at the end of most sections. Some tasks are merely for practice purposes, but every so often you will need to carry out the 'Self-check' and to make your 'Progress report'.

CARRYING OUT THE 'SELF-CHECK'

After the practice materials on each item, there is a 'self-check' section, which will help you to develop your accuracy. It is a good idea to carry out a set routine after completing each piece of work. Not only will this help you to prepare for the exam, but it will get you into the habit of carefully checking all the work that you produce once you are employed as a typist.

The 'self-check' procedure

1   When you have completed a task from the practice material, check it to see if you have mastered the item that you were covering. (Each self-check includes a list of special points to help you to do this.)
2   Read your work a second time to spot errors in words not in the special points list.
3   Make corrections to your work as necessary (see pages 104 - 5 for information on correcting).
4   Pass your work to someone else to see if that person can spot any errors. This person may be a typewriting teacher or a friend or relative who is prepared to read your work and may be able to see any errors you missed.

THE ROYAL SOCIETY OF ARTS EXAMINATIONS BOARD

SINGLE-SUBJECT EXAMINATIONS

A185
TYPEWRITING SKILLS
STAGE I (Elementary)
WEDNESDAY 6 NOVEMBER 1985

(TIME ALLOWED — TWO HOURS)

Notes for Candidates

1 Please type your name and centre number on each piece of your work.

2 Please assemble your completed work in the order in which it is presented in this paper and cross through any work which you do not wish to be marked.

3 Calculators and English dictionaries may be used in the examinations.

_____

You must:

1 Complete all tasks.

2 Use only the stationery provided in your answer book.

3 Insert today's date on letters and memos, unless otherwise instructed.

(Penalties will be incurred if these instructions are not followed.)

TSI(Autumn)   © R.S.A. 1985

CHECKING YOUR PROGRESS

Once you have had your work checked by someone else, you will need to keep a progress report on which items and practice material you have covered.

The example below shows how you should rule up a sheet of paper and the headings to be used for your progress report:

Syllabus Item No	Task No	Errors found by Checker	Target date for accurate repeat	Date completed without error
B1/2	1	(1) Linton 4 typing: r for t overtype; m for n; z for v (2) typing b for v; blank — forgot to fill in after correcting	10/3/86 14/3/86	
	2			14/3/86

(a) (b) (c)

If the person checking your work found no errors, enter the date in column (c) as a record that the work has been completed without error.

If that person found errors in your work, even though you thought it was accurate, you should:

1 list in column (a) the errors found;
2 write in column (b) a date by which you hope to be able to complete the work again and this time have no errors found by someone else;
3 re-type the practice material, carry out the self-check again and then pass to your 'checker' – and, if necessary, make further entries in columns (a) and (b) in your diary;
4 enter the completion date in column (c) once your 'checker' finds no errors.

NEW SCHEME FOR TYPEWRITING SKILLS STAGE I

THIS FORM – FOR USE IN WORKING TASK 6 – MUST BE INSERTED INSIDE THE COVER OF YOUR ANSWER BOOK AT THE CONCLUSION OF THE EXAMINATION. IF BOTH SIDES OF THIS FORM ARE USED ONE ATTEMPT MUST BE CANCELLED.

ORDER

ORDER NO.

VILLIERS ENGINEERING

25 GREEN STREET

LONDON   NW4 6XL

TO	DATE

CODE NO.	QTY.	DESCRIPTION	UNIT PRICE £	PRICE £	P
				TOTAL £	

SIGNED

FOR EXPORT

When you are working as a typist no one will tell you to put the date on letters and memos. Your boss will expect you to know this and to remember to do it, using today's date unless told otherwise.

The test is: *will you remember, and will you get it right?*

'HOUSE' STYLES

Your employer may have a particular style that you will need to follow. This may simply be your employer's preference, or it may be to fit pre-printed stationery, for example, all in figures to fit into a small printed box; because it is quicker; or because it is the custom and practice where you work, such as in a hospital.

Here are seven different ways to type the date:

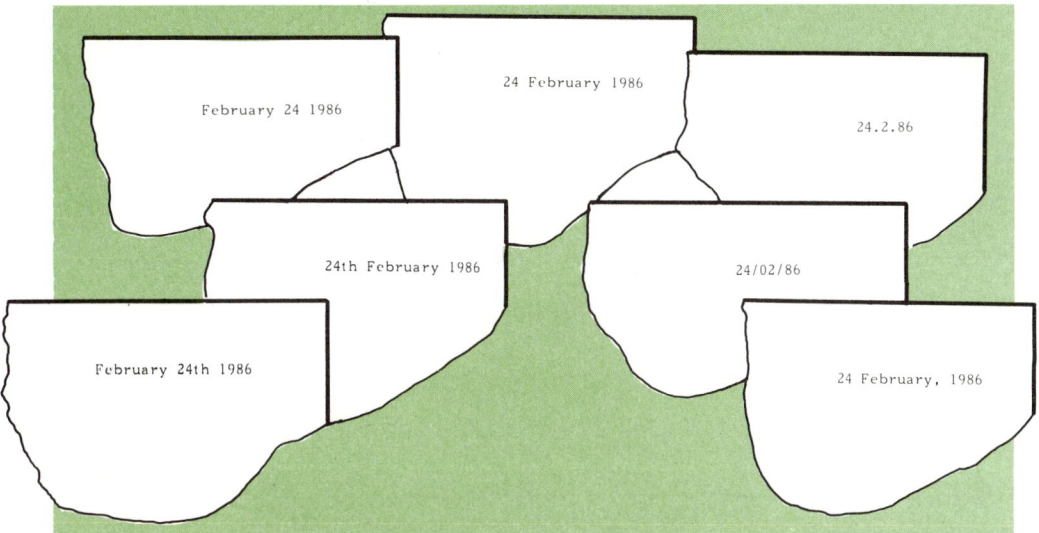

February 24 1986

24 February 1986

24.2.86

24th February 1986

24/02/86

February 24th 1986

24 February, 1986

It is not generally accepted practice for the day or the year in a document date to be typed in words like this:

The twenty-fourth of February nineteen hundred and eighty-six

WHERE TO TYPE THE DATE

Most people seem to prefer to type the date at the left margin, while others like to see it on the right of letterheads:

PRAXITELES GROUP
A fictitious organisation for examination purposes only

PRAXITELES HOUSE · ADAM STREET · LONDON WC2N 6EZ
TELEPHONE 01 930 5115

Our ref

Your ref

24 February 1986 — *equally acceptable*

most popular choice — 24 February 1986

Typist:
Complete the order form.

Order No: 62
To: AB Lighting plc
       16 Stratford Rd.
       LONDON   EC4A 6LE

Code No	Qty	Description	Unit Price £	Price £ P
3A80	2	Light sockets 2¼ in × 1 in	5.15	10 30

Total £ 10 30

The date must be clearly set apart from the rest of the letter, that is, with at least one clear line space above and below it.

Some stationery includes a printed heading 'Date' to remind you to date the document, as well as to show you where it should be typed. It is very important not to overtype such a pre-printed heading or any dotted lines (see also C12 on page 106); nor should you type the word 'Date' yourself, whether or not it is pre-printed.

IN THE EXAM

An instruction is given on the front of the test paper:

'Insert today's date on letters and memos'

If dates are required on other tasks, special instructions will be given in the individual task details.

The stationery for *letters* provided by the RSA does not have a printed heading 'Date' to show you where to type the date. You may type it in any position so long as it is treated as a separate item and can be clearly seen with a minimum of one clear line space above and below it. In the exam the position of the date is not related to any particular style of layout of letters.

Memo forms do have a heading 'date' and you should use the variable line-spacer or the interliner to line up your printing point with the printed heading. Leave a minimum of one clear space after the heading before typing the date.

There are no rules about how to type the date. You may use any style other than all words – *but you must be consistent*. Once you have decided which way you are going to type the date, stick to it: if other dates occur in the same document, be careful to type them in the same style.

Remember

Dates can be very important:

- make sure you date all letters and memos;
- make sure the date is accurate.

WHAT THE EXAMINER WILL LOOK FOR

Accuracy

! inaccuracy or omission of any part of the date (day, month or year)
! typing in the word 'Date'

Presentation

√ same style throughout a task
√ clear line above and below the date
√ entries on the same line as pre-printed headings
√ entries not overtyping the dotted lines on forms or the pre-printed headings on forms

Memo

From Manager To Purchasing Officer [please retain abbreviations]

Shirley's Bathroom Accessories Inc, Virginia, USA.

Further to your memo of Tuesday 11 June 1985 I confirm that we have now recd. suff. customer enquiries to ~~warrant~~ justify the placement of an order to the States for:

Six jacuzzis, model no 821B, size 7 ft x 7 ft at a wholesale price of $5500 each and seven sauna room kits, model no 6167E, size 8 ft x 6 ft, with the 45° angle shower head attachment, at $5950 each.

Inset 5 spaces

It wd. be appreciated if delivery could be arranged for approx. 1 ~~July~~ September 1985 to our warehouse in Rochdale. ~~Bath~~ Please order a variety of colours – perhaps a ~~variety~~ mixture of mulberry red, avocado green and sienna brown would be suitable?

When working in an office, or typing letters for yourself, you will often need to find or check details from previous correspondence, from files in a cabinet or on a microcomputer or from a database such as Ceefax or Oracle.

When people prepare drafts in handwriting they often take short-cuts and after they have written items such as names, they may leave the typist to fill in the same names when they are repeated. For example:

IN THE EXAM

You will not be asked to invent or to supply any information, but you will be expected to be able to fill in details from work in the exam paper.

The 'repeats' that need to be completed will appear in the same task.

To help you at least the first letter of each word will be given, as in the examples above.

WHAT THE EXAMINER WILL LOOK FOR

Accuracy

√   the right words, accurately typed

B1 – B2 *Practice material*

1   Copy the three personal business letters for Mr Johnson.
2   Fill in a progress report

TASK 4

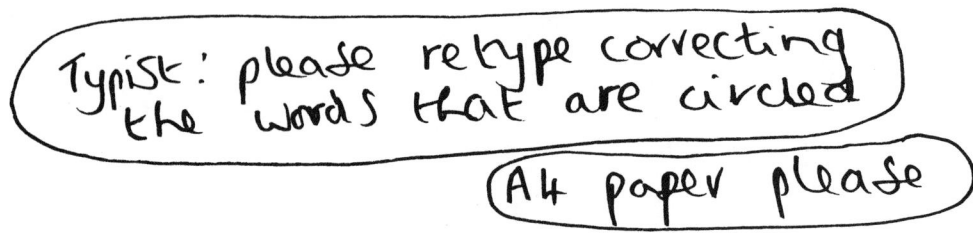

Typist: please retype correcting the words that are circled

A4 paper please

WHY WAS STONEHENGE BUILT?

Although we know something of the various parts
of Stonehenge, such as how and when it was
built, we know very little about why it was built.
There are no written records because nobody in
Britain could write until they were taught by
the Romans more than 1500 years after the final
stones were hoisted into place at the end of
the Bronze Age about 1550 BC.

It is thought by most people that Stonehenge was
some kind of temple, but no-one knows for sure
which gods were worshipped. Some think that
Stonehenge was built by the Druids, but this is
certainly not so. From writers like Julius Caesar,
we know that the Druids were priests in England
and France during the last two or three centuries
B C and by then Stonehenge had been standing for
more than 1000 years and were probably already a
ruin. A man named John aubrey invented the idea
of a Druids' temple only three centuries ago in
the first detailed account of Stonehenge. All
we do know is that the huge circle of natural
stone's was used for some kind of prehistoric
worship.

43 Linston Terrace
Fennyman Street
Sheffield S4 3LT

F D Hope Esq
Sales Director
Praxiteles Group
Adam Street
London WC2N 6EZ

Dear Mr H——

My neighbour, Mr J Janison of 41 L—— T——, has recommended that I contact you for details of the nearest stockist of your product, 'Praxiwrap' Loft Insulation. Your previous agents in this town, J + D Bix of Main Street, Sh——, have moved away.

Yours faithfully

James Johnson

Mr B D Smithie
43 Church Lane
Bentwood
Yorkshire   S9 4JD

43 L—— T——
F—— St
Sheffield S4 3LT

Dear Mr Smithie

Thank you for your letter + telephone call regarding the completion of work at my house + supply of material for loft in——.

My neighbour, Mr Janison of 41 L—— T——, has recommended 'Praxiwrap', but I have been unable to locate the supplier. I have today written to Mr Hope, Sales Dir—— of Praxi— G—— in London, + will contact you again when he replies.

Yours faithfully

J—— J——

TASK 3

TYPIST:
Display on A5 paper with the shorter edge at the top

THE PAVILION THEATRE ← Type in spaced caps

SHOWS FOR CHILDREN – JULY 1985
Every Saturday morning at 11.30 am

6 Jul.
PIETRO'S PUPPETS
A ↓ funny performance about a bear
and a mouse. fascinating and
5-9 years

20 Jul.
$2 + 2 = 5^2$
A class of schoolchildren finds a new way
of learning arithmetic.
7-12 years

13 Jul.
FEET-FIRST
An interesting journey to the forest.
3-7 years

27 Jul.
HULA
A new dance-theatre show.
7-11 years

For full details of these and other
programmes, contact the Box Office,
The Pavilion Theatre, Cheadle-on-Sea.
Telephone 62417.

43 L— T—
F—
Sheffield S4 —

Mr T Jenkins
28 Manton Avenue
BINGLEY
Yorkshire
BY4 8SF

Dear Tom

Do you know whether 'Praxiwrap' L—9—— is the best possible product for use in a house such as mine? My neighbour, Mr J—— of 41 L— T——, has recommended it.

Even if it is the best, I cannot trace the local stockist, although I have written to the Sales Dir—— of the manufacturers & hope to hear soon.

If you would advise another make I would like to know.

Thank you.

Best wishes

TASK 2

Typist : leave a 50mm (2") top margin

Type heading in closed caps

The East/West balance of computers

Type in double (or 1½) line spacing

This table shows that the development of computers in Russia and Eastern Europe has been ~~very much~~ far slower than ~~that~~ in the West:

Country	Population (millions)	Number of computers
WEST		
USA	211.9	168,800
Japan	109.7	30,095
UK	56.2	15,520
West Germany	62.0	20,860
France	52.5	13,064
TOTAL	492.3	248,339
EAST		
USSR	252.1	12,500
Eastern Europe*	104.8	2,935
TOTAL	356.9	15,435

December 1977 figures

* East Germany, Poland, Czechoslovakia, Hungary, Rumania, Bulgaria

SELF-CHECK

Special points

1 Did you remember to date each letter accurately, with the date on which you typed it?
2 Did you find the facts to complete the blanks in each letter? These were:

Task 1

Hope
Linston Terrace
Sheffield

Task 2

Linston Terrace
Fennyman Street
insulation
Linston Terrace
Director
Praxiteles Group
James Johnson

Task 3

Linston Terrace
Fennyman Street
S4 3LT
Loft Insulation
Janison (*or* J. Janison)
Linston Terrace
Director

PROGRESS REPORT

Read your work carefully for typing errors. Make corrections and then pass it to someone else to check. When you get it back, fill in your progress report (see page 11).

TASK 1

(Typist: carbon copy and envelope please)

Our ref AJB/pw
Mr A Timms
16 Railway Terrace
Rochester Kent
RO6 7PJ

(Please mark Confidential)

Dear Mr T_____

<u>Life Assurance Policy No 813469/T/141</u>
Thank you for yr. letter dated Monday, 10 June 1985 requesting a quotation for an additional to your existing policy in the form of a Personal Pension Plan.

current
Our / records show that you are 41 years of age & we have pleasure in enclosing our recommended plan, the terms of wh. wl. apply provided that the policy comes into force before your next birthday. // We also publish a leaflet giving full details of the scheme and your attention is drawn to the section on bonus figures. We must advise you that there is not guarantee of the bonus rate as we cannot foresee what percentage will be granted in future years, but the example shown on our quotation illustrates bonuses at present rates.

from you

We look forward to hearing when you have had an opp. to peruse these details and please do not hesitate to let us know if we can be of help furthers.

Yours sincerely

Alan Breeze
Pensions Manager

140

Some of the handwritten work that you could be given to type in an office may look difficult because of crossed-out words and other amendments. If you are not used to dealing with this kind of work you may make keyboarding errors or find that it takes you longer to complete the job.

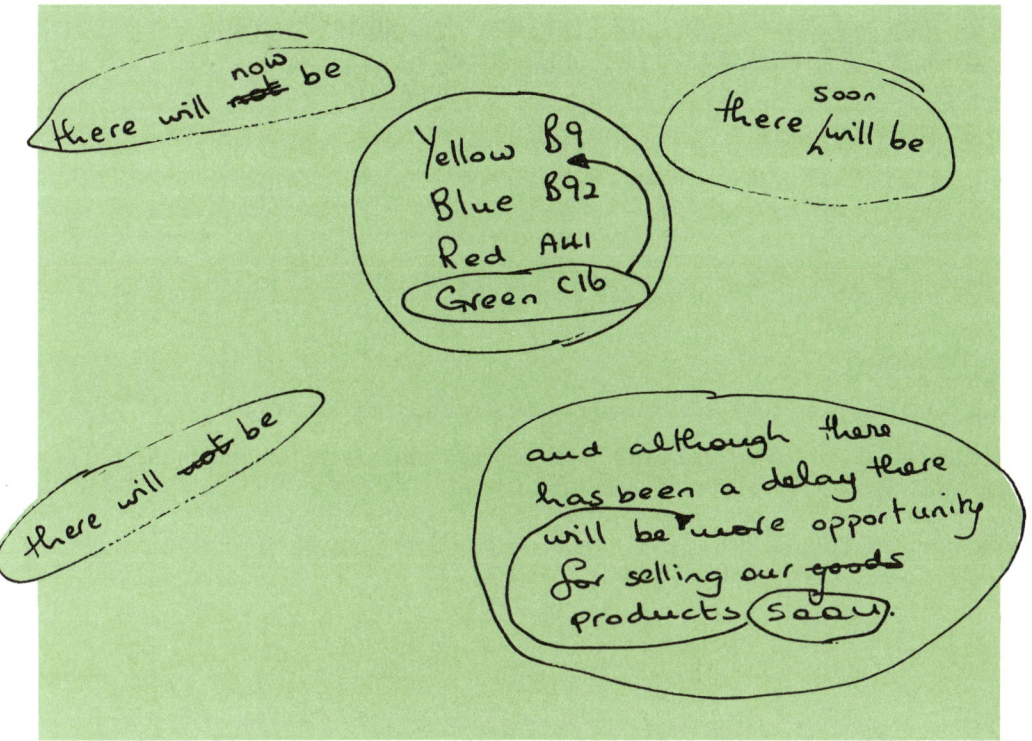

Amendments to text, such as those shown above, are not difficult to understand. They are simple instructions asking you to make minor alterations. The only 'signs' used are the marks to *add* (or insert) a word or to move text.

SIGNS YOU NEED TO KNOW

Paragraphs

The sign asking you to start a new paragraph can either look like this [or like this //.

i.e.   to be typed as:

We are going to be there. [We hope to see you soon.	We are going to be there. We hope to see you soon.

or

We are going to be there. // We hope to see you soon.

THE ROYAL SOCIETY OF ARTS
EXAMINATIONS BOARD
SINGLE-SUBJECT EXAMINATIONS

187 NEW SCHEME FOR TYPEWRITING SKILLS STAGE I - PILOT
THURSDAY, 13th JUNE 1985

[TIME ALLOWED - TWO HOURS]

Notes for Candidates

1   Please type your name and centre number on each piece of your work.

2   Please assemble your completed work in the order in which it is presented in this paper and cross through any work which you do not wish to be marked.

3   Calculators and English dictionaries may be used in the examinations.

You must:

1   Complete all tasks.

2   Use only the stationery provided in your answer book.

3   Insert today's date on letters and memos, unless otherwise instructed.

(Penalties will be incurred if these instructions are not followed.)

TSI(PILOT)   © RSA 1985

Sometimes the writer may decide not to start a new paragraph where there was one before, but to 'run on' from the previous paragraph. The run on sign looks like this ⌐

i.e.   to be typed as:

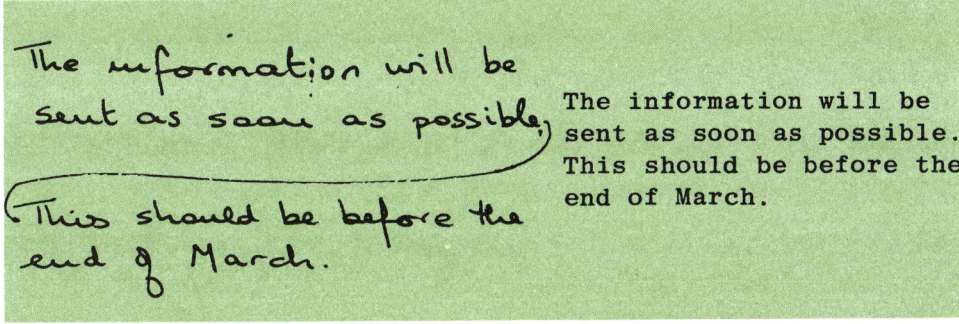

The information will be
sent as soon as possible.
This should be before the
end of March.

Transposing items

Words or items may need to change places (to be transposed). The signs you need to know are: ⌣⌐ , ↻↺ , [ ] .

i.e.   to be typed as:

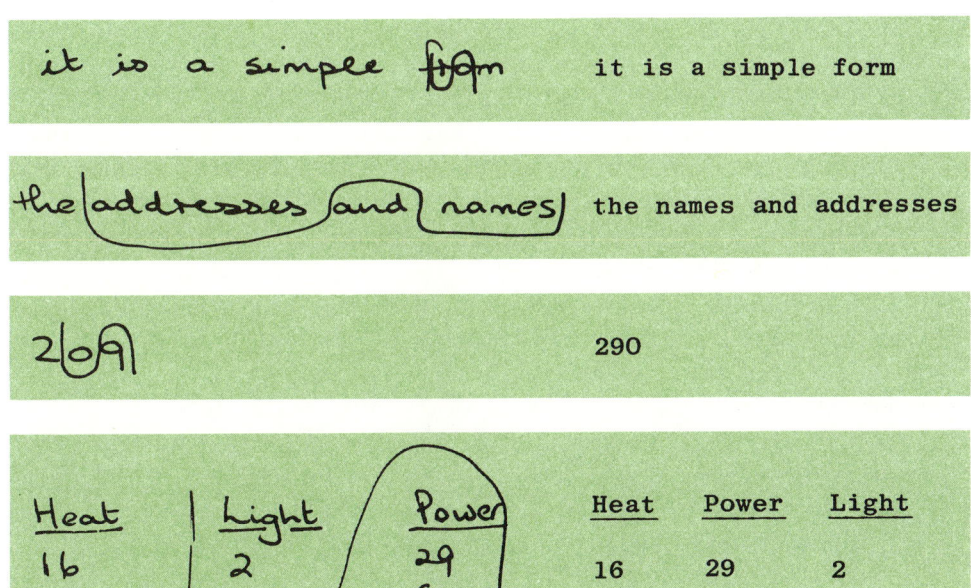

it is a simple form

the names and addresses

290

Heat	Power	Light
16	29	2
12	81	4
14	34	8
4	46	7

Colour	Stock No
Green	B9
Blue	C16
Red	A41
Yellow	B92

GENERAL CHECKING PROCEDURE

1 Use the syllabus and the marking scheme to check you have fulfilled Objectives B1, B3, B5 – B8 and C1 – C12. For instance, did you date the letter and memo as required by Objective B1? If not, the marking scheme tells you (see B2.1) the omission of these three words must be counted as three word faults.

   Did you leave at least one clear line between paragraphs, and the same number each time in tasks, as required by Objectives C10 and C3?

2 Look back at the exam paper to check you have included every instruction and amendment in your work.

3 Now check the points for Objectives B2, B4 and B9 in the special points check list on page 00. Included in the checklist are notes on one or two points about which you may have had to make decisions.

4 Note the errors you find. Distinguish between word and presentation faults so that you can eventually count the number of faults in each class to see if you would have passed.

5 Finally, read through each task very carefully for typographical errors or wrong words you have not yet noticed.

6 Count your faults. To pass, you must have no more than fourteen word faults and no more than nine presentation faults. With no more than five word faults and no more than five presentation faults you would get a distinction.

7 Plan how you are going to remedy your faults. Group your faults under the headings: 'Keyboarding'; 'misunderstanding or misreading' and 'forgetting'.

   If you make several errors in *keyboarding*, spend some time each day copying material in Part Three. Aim to type longer each time before making an error – but do not give up if you make a mistake. Instead, make corrections so that at the end of the time you have allocated for practice, your work is free of error.

   If your faults are due to *misunderstanding or misreading* it means that you must take extra time to read through drafts rather than scanning, and to check meanings *before* you start typing tasks.

   Forgetting is some people's biggest fault. Make notes to remind yourself, for example, to return to the margin after an inset, to type the rest of a sentence after inserting words in a 'balloon', to take a copy, to type an envelope. A red pen might help here, so that you can highlight instructions for yourself on the exam paper.

The 'stet' sign

Sometimes the writer will cross out a word, and after writing in a new word, decide the original one was better and so cross out the new word as well. It is important then to be sure which word has to be typed. This is shown by writing a broken line under the correct item. Because this sort of amendment can be confusing and needs extra care, a circled tick is written in the margin to draw your attention to this.

i.e.   to be typed as:

⊘ The ~~company~~ ~~business~~ concerned will pay	The company concerned will pay
⊘ there are, ~~we believe you~~ ~~as you already~~ ~~told us~~, ~~know~~ two	there are, as you already know, two

	Benches	Stools	Chairs	Benches	Stools	Chairs
⊘	14210	~~19365~~ 17284	12822	14 210 29 984	19 365 8 662	12 822 44 987
⊘	29984	8662	~~44987~~ ~~52300~~			

IN THE EXAM

In the exam any of the amendments shown in this chapter, and in the syllabus (see pages 3 – 4), may be included in any of the tasks. If there is not enough space for new words to be added in their right place these may have to appear in the margin. Otherwise there will be *no* reminder signs in the margin, *except* where an item has been crossed out and then marked with a circled tick and dotted line.

Remember

Reading carefully through the wording will help you to see easily what is required.

Most typists understand amendment signs, but often *forget* to carry out the instructions properly or, after the alteration has been made, *forget* to go back to the unaltered script and put in the next words correctly.

WHAT THE EXAMINER WILL LOOK FOR

Accuracy

! words not altered as shown by the amendment, including paragraphing amendment(s)
! words not moved to place shown by amendment
! words moved properly, but typed inaccurately

Note:
No word will be penalised twice for inaccuracy.

Presentation

√ Paragraphing shown consistently throughout, including any new paragraphs asked for by handwritten amendments

Part Four

Exam Practice:
Preparing for RSA
Typewriting Skills Stage I

In the exam you will be asked to complete six tasks. These will include a:

1   letter;
2   memorandum;
3   pre-printed form to be completed with given information;
4   notice, advertisement, etc.;
5   three-column table with single-line headings;
6   piece of continuous text, such as an article, extract, etc.

As part of these six tasks, you will be expected to type one envelope and one carbon copy.

The two specimen exam papers included here will help you to complete your preparations. They are followed by a special points checklist to guide you when checking your work.

USING THE SPECIMEN EXAM PAPERS

1   Create an examination atmosphere for yourself:

* avoid scanning the practice papers in advance;
* fix a day and time when you will test yourself. Arrange to have two hours without interruption;
* use a special folder for your practice exam work. Collect your stationery (as listed in paragraph 4.3 of the syllabus and Chapter C1) including letter and memo paper and the relevant form. In the exam you will be provided with an envelope, but for practice work you must supply your own.

2   On the day:

* organise your work area with stationery: including carbon paper; pencil and pen (preferably black); soft rubber; typewriting eraser, correcting fluid and/or coated correcting paper; material (small piece of paper, card or thin plastic) to protect carbon copy while correcting;
* have tissues handy;
* make sure you wear a watch or can see a clock.

3   After completing your 'mock' exam:

* wait until the next day before checking your work so that you can take a fresh look at instructions and spot errors more easily;
* take the check procedure seriously (see below). Allocate time for it in the same way as for your typing. *Remember*, the purpose of completing a specimen exam paper is to judge if you are likely to pass the exam *and* to find any weaknesses you must remedy.

Task 4

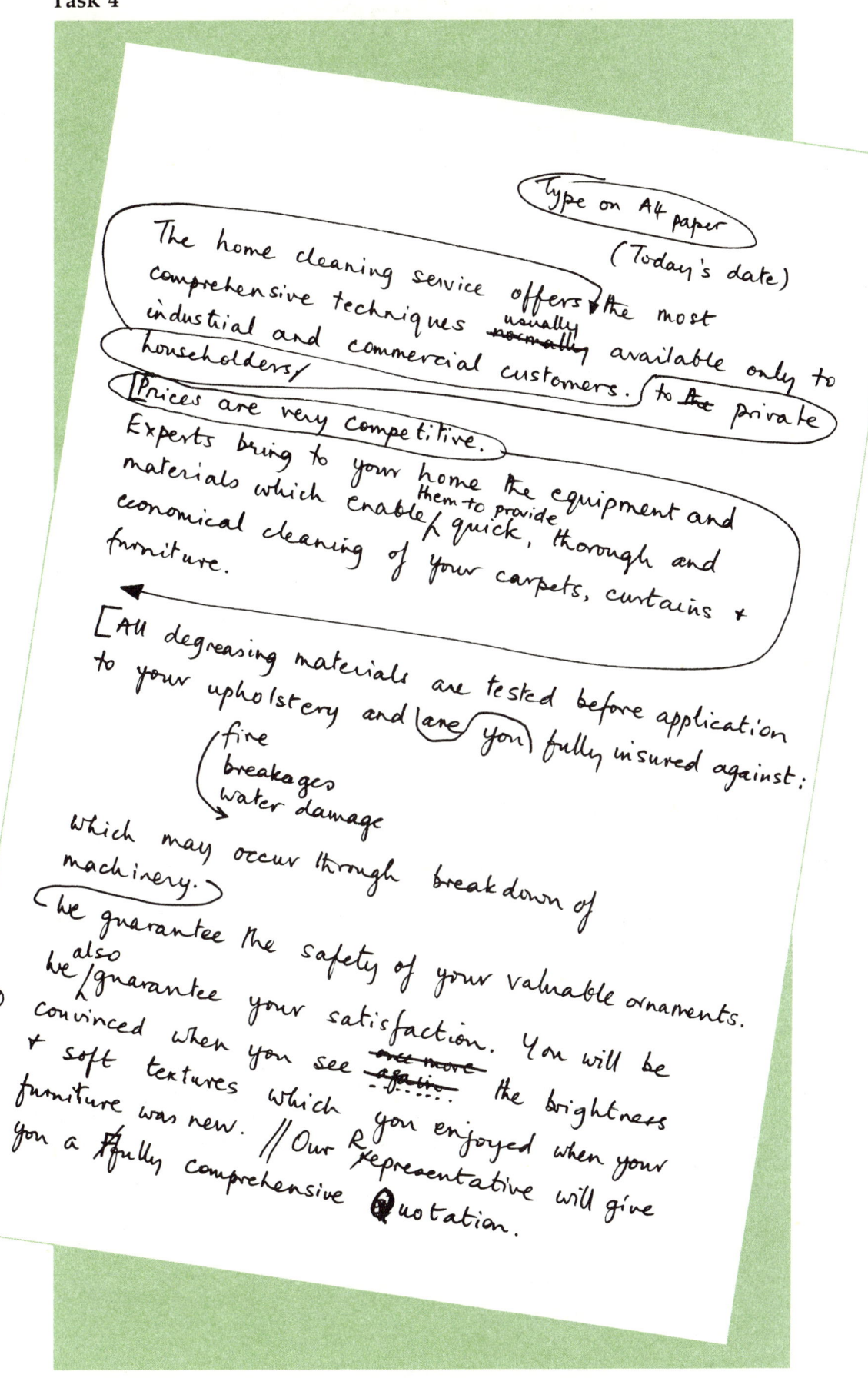

Suggested time allowance: 23 minutes

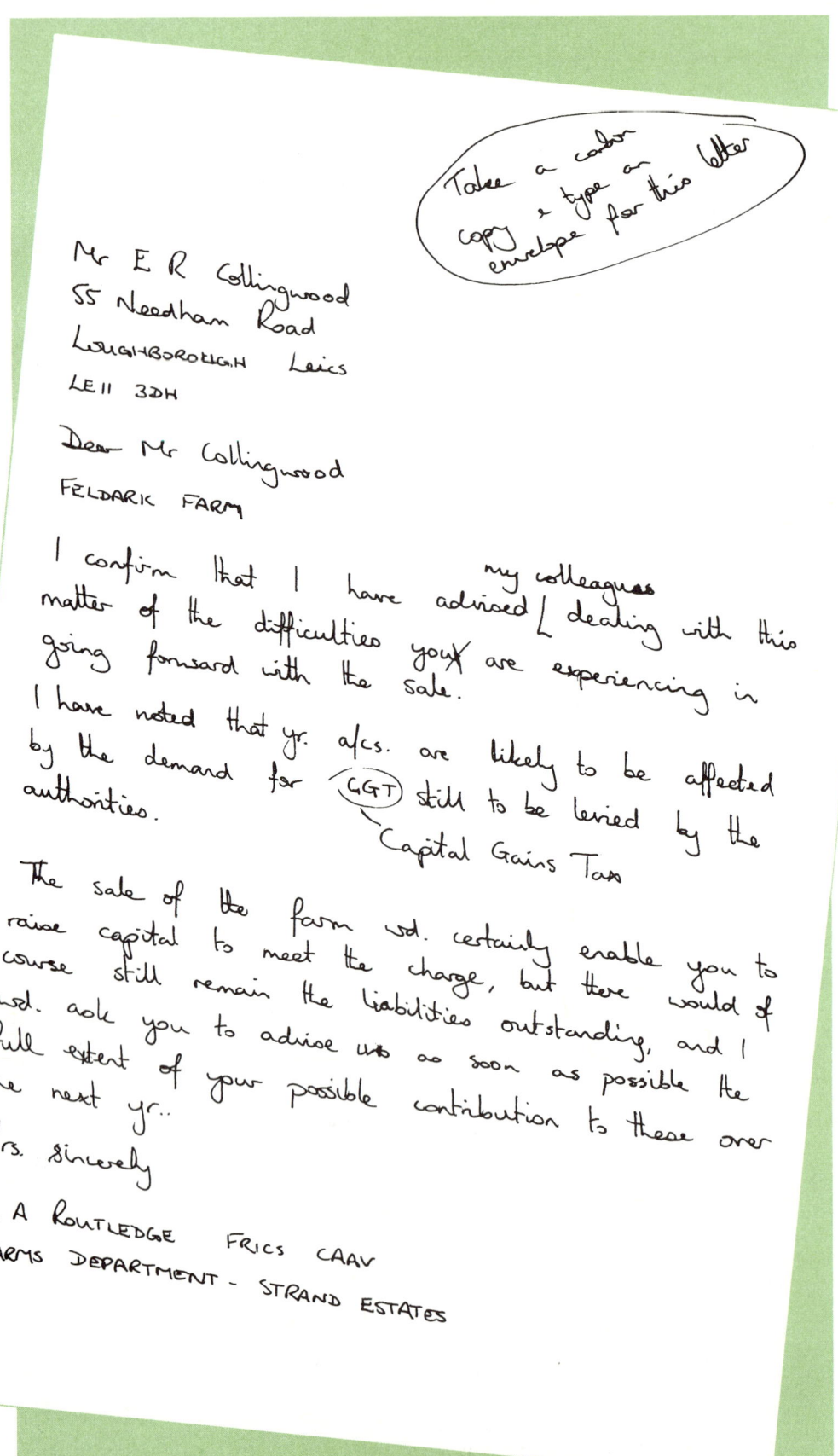

Take a carbon copy & type an envelope for this letter

Mr E R Collingwood
55 Needham Road
LOUGHBOROUGH Leics
LE11 3DH

Dear Mr Collingwood
FELDARK FARM

I confirm that I have advised my colleagues dealing with this matter of the difficulties you are experiencing in going forward with the sale.

I have noted that yr. a/cs. are likely to be affected by the demand for CGT still to be levied by the authorities. — Capital Gains Tax

The sale of the farm wd. certainly enable you to raise capital to meet the charge, but there would of course still remain the liabilities outstanding, and I wd. ask you to advise us as soon as possible the full extent of your possible contribution to these over the next yr..

Yrs. sincerely

R A ROUTLEDGE FRICS CAAV
FARMS DEPARTMENT - STRAND ESTATES

B3 *Practice material: self-check and progress report*

SELF-CHECK

Special points

1 Did you date the document accurately?
2 Make sure that you carried out all the amendments properly, by checking your typed work against the following:

The home cleaning service offers to private householders the most comprehensive techniques usually available only to industrial and commercial customers.

Experts bring to your home the equipment and materials which enable them to provide quick, thorough and economical cleaning of your carpets, curtains and furniture.

Prices are very competitive.

All degreasing materials are tested before application to your upholstery and you are fully insured against:

    breakages
    water damage
    fire

which may occur through breakdown of machinery. We guarantee the safety of your valuable ornaments.

We also guarantee your satisfaction. You will be convinced when you see again the brightness and soft textures which you enjoyed when your furniture was new.

Our Representative will give you a fully comprehensive Quotation.

Note:
It is not an error if you typed the task in double-line spacing.

PROGRESS REPORT

Read your work carefully for typing errors. Make corrections and then pass it to someone else to check. When you get it back, fill in your progress report (see page 11).

Suggested time allowance: 12 minutes

Denville and Partners
Chamberlain House
Derry Road
FAIRLAWNS Hants
B41 8QT

Envelope required

Dear Sirs

We have now received your undated letter calling for delivery of your Order No 2876/B.

Unfortunately we do not appear to have received your order, and as we notice in your final paragraph your refer to "Light Fittings", are doubtful if the Order would have been sent to us as we do not supply these items.

Perhaps you will check your records to make sure we are concerned, + if so provide us with further details to enable us to trace the matter.

Yours flly.

Manager

Spelling

TYPING ABBREVIATIONS IN FULL

We wd. recom. that sep. accom. be provided & bel. this wl. be arranged.

When you type any correspondence or other documents – whether for yourself or in a job – people reading your work will quickly notice your spelling mistakes. Even though a letter may have been checked and signed by someone else, it is usually the typist who is blamed for spelling errors.

You cannot expect to know how to spell every word, but it is your responsibility to check that your work is accurate. Typists in a company using specialist and technical language could expect to be given a list of difficult spellings.

A dictionary will not, of course, help if you do not know the word to look for; nor can you afford the time to look up too many words. You can improve your spelling by reading more carefully, not being content to skip words, and generally paying attention to words and their meanings. As a typist, words are what you work with most. A typist who is not interested in words is like a hairdresser not interested in hair, or a motor mechanic who hates cars.

Dr. Dr Stone

We ack. rec. of yr. letter regarding yr. insurance claim in Jan. of last yr.

Only by reading carefully for the meaning of words will you be able to make the right choice of word when abbreviations have been used. In the example above the abbreviation 'yr.' is used for both 'year' and 'your'; 'Dr' stands for 'Dear', and needs to be typed in full, and 'Doctor', which should be typed as abbreviated, i.e. Dear Dr Stone.

IN THE EXAM

Technical words are not deliberately included – but, of course, some words may appear technical to some people and not to others. All names will be written as clearly as possible.

& although we are sure you wl. find Praxigro useful our other range of Praxisewings wl. be ever more effective

VACANCIES IN THE ADMINISTRATIVE SECTION

With the installationof new systems and equipment there will
be xeveral vacancies occurring for senior staff, as well as
openings for supervisors and operators.

During the next few weeks we shall found that we are all
inconveneinced through alterations, removal of older equipment
and istallation of word processing and computerised files.
Most of the people who will be taking an active part in intro-
ducing the new systems and taking over the work of the company
temporarily are alweady aware of the procedures to be followed
and how it will affect their work schedules. For others,
meetngs will be held on Tuesday and Thurday of next week and
lists of those who are expected to attend are now posted on the
notice boards.

As soon as you have the full details and realise what contribution
you can make you should make application for any post(s) in
wich you are interested.

The posts is to be advertised in local newspapers next month.

You are allowed to use a dictionary in the exam.

We asked groups of employers, teachers and senior secretaries which words they found most commonly misspelt and on page 4 you will find a list of these. Some of these words will be used in each exam. They will be abbreviated, to give you the chance to show that you can spell them correctly. Although you may use a dictionary to check them it would help you to memorise this list so that you can deal with these words quickly and correctly when they appear.

All abbreviated words that are to be spelt out in full are followed by a full stop, except for (a) the handwritten sign for 'and', which should also be typed in full in sentences, although it must be copied if shown in company names, and (b) the word 'through' which is abbreviated with an apostrophe, 'thro''.

Spelling is tested only in this way. There are no deliberate spelling mistakes in the exam at Stage I. You should copy accurately all unabbreviated words, using a dictionary if you need to.

Remember

Look for the full stop to indicate words that must be typed in full from the abbreviation. For example:

Handwritten	Typed
Hon Sec.	Hon Secretary
Rev E J Marshall	Rev E J Marshall
Dr. Sirs	Dear Sirs
Dr F Moore	Dr F Moore
this yr. & next yr.	this year and next year
& yr. A/c. No is 2468	and your Account No is 2468
Messrs Jones & Blokes Ltd	Messrs Jones & Blokes Ltd
Messrs Jones and Blokes Ltd,.	Messrs Jones and Blokes Limited.

An abbreviated word at the end of a sentence will have two full stops to show that it should be typed out in full (see above).

Suggested time allowance: 25 minutes

PRAXITELES GROUP

Fine Art Department

(By instructions from Executors and local vendors)

SALE BY AUCTION - (spaced caps)

Leave space here at least 64mm x 75mm (2½" x 3")

at

WESTGATE HALL SALEROOMS

CAMBRIDGE

on

Wed.

14 MAY 1986

at 10 am

Antique furniture including a Victorian credenza, a
set of six Victorian balloon-backed ~~chars~~, a Dutch   dining chairs
floral marquetry chest of drawers. Studio and Art
pottery, porcelain, metalware, silver and plated ware,
paintings, prints and books. A small collection of
cigarette cards. A large quantity of English coins
etc.

VIEWING: Tues. ~~15~~ 13 May 1986 - 11.30 am to 4.30 pm

CATALOGUES: £1 ~~pp~~ from the Auctioneers' offices,
Westgate Hall, CAMBRIDGE, CB2 6PF
(Tel: 0223 - 64720)

ABBREVIATIONS TO BE TYPED

You should *not* alter abbreviations used in names, such as,

  Miss Ms Mrs Mr Messrs The Rt Hon Dr Rev Esq

or for Latin words, such as,

    etc   et al   viz   eg   ie

IN THE EXAM

These words will not be followed by a full stop, unless they appear at the end of a sentence, where there would normally be punctuation.

  Typing in full a word that should remain abbreviated will be penalised as a word fault – even though it may be spelt correctly.

WHAT THE EXAMINER WILL LOOK FOR

Accuracy

! no greater or smaller penalties apply to errors caused by poor spelling than any other cause – any wrong word is counted as a fault
! typing in full words that should be left as abbreviations, even if you spell these correctly – a word fault will be counted if you type, for example, 'Mister J Jones' or 'et cetera'

B4 *Practice material*

Task 5

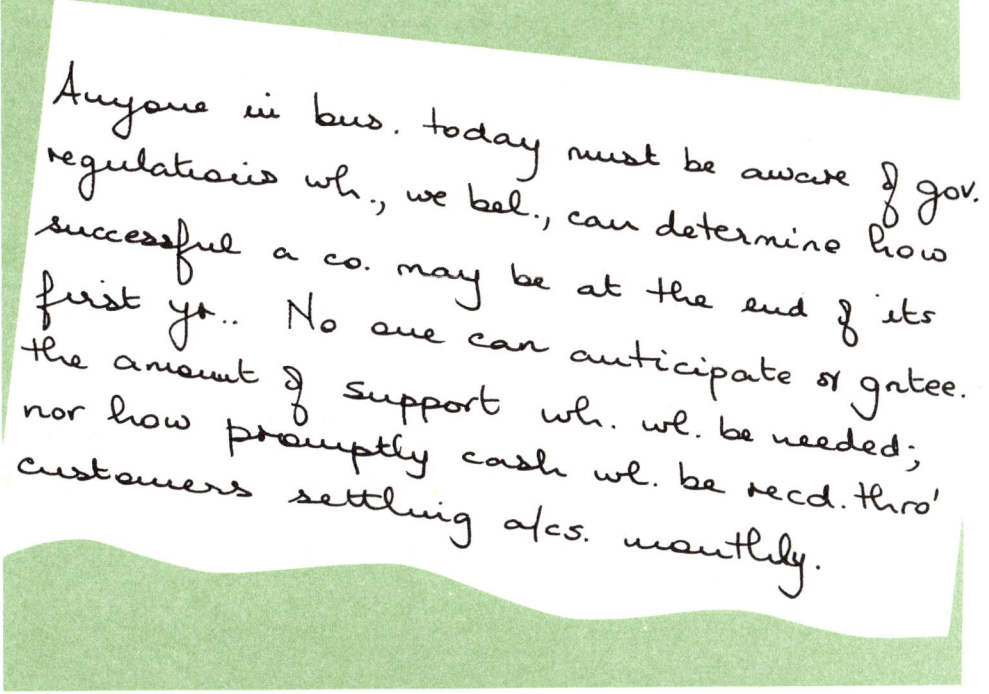

Suggested time allowance: 20 minutes

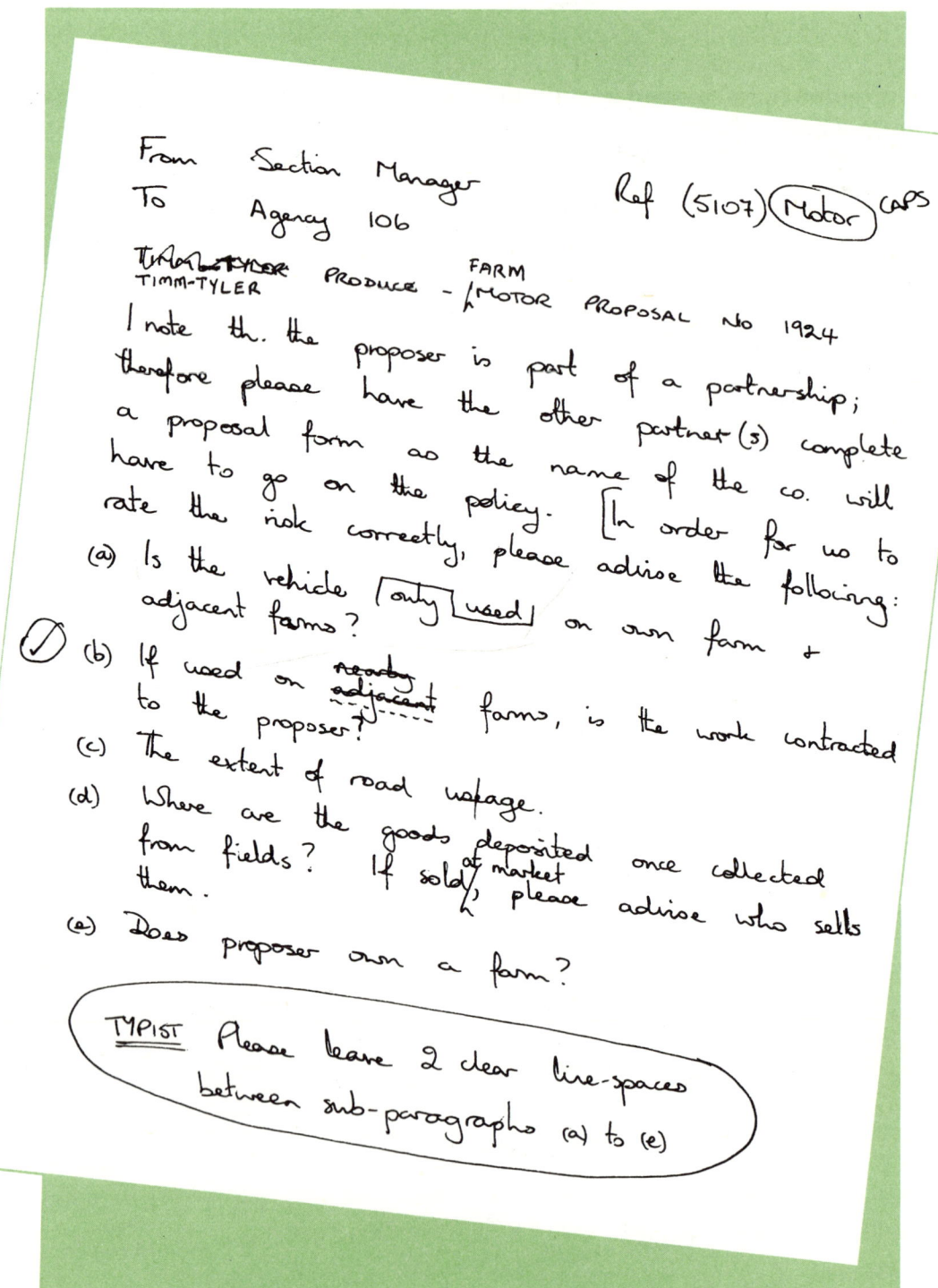

From Section Manager   Ref (5107) (Motor) CAPS

To Agency 106

~~TIMM-TYLER~~ TIMM-TYLER PRODUCE - FARM /MOTOR PROPOSAL No 1924

I note th. the proposer is part of a partnership; therefore please have the other partner(s) complete a proposal form as the name of the co. will have to go on the policy. [In order for us to rate the risk correctly, please advise the following:

(a) Is the vehicle [only used] on own farm + adjacent farms?

(b) If used on ~~nearby~~ ~~adjacent~~ farms, is the work contracted to the proposer?

(c) The extent of road usage.

(d) Where are the goods deposited once collected from fields? If sold at market, please advise who sells them.

(e) Does proposer own a farm?

TYPIST Please leave 2 clear line-spaces between sub-paragraphs (a) to (e)

We ack. that it has been incon. for everyone involved in the road repairs in Daisytown Cres.. Certain householders did exp. difficulties whilst the temp. surface was in use. The matter was ref'd. to the manager, who gave suff. instructions wh. were ~~fty~~ properly carried out. Although misc. items are outstanding, the whole ex. is well on the way to completion.

Task 7

It is apptox. 6 months since your appt. as clerk-typist and it wl. be necy. next month to arrange for you to rec. exps. You wl. be resp. for 2 sep. types of purchase and I sh. reqm. that you send in recs. for money paid by you so that immed. repayment can be made. The system must def. be complied w. if delays are to be avoided.

payment & co.

Suggested time allowance: 20 minutes

Our ref. No 6831

Mrs B Lewis

2 The Grove

MINSTER

Kent

CT8 3RP

Envelope + copy required

Dear Mrs Lewis

Further to our telephone conversation concerning the Travel Policy wh. we are arranging for you w the Lloyd's Underwriters, please find enclosed Certificate wh. underwriters have issued.

No. TR128513

You will note that the premium amounts to £37.20 // No doubt you will let us have a remittance in due course

for this amount

Yrs. sdy.

John Rodgers

Hastings Administrative Office

The co. will be issuing a new cat. for the autumn and this wl. represent a new form of marketing. ~~The~~ In previous yrs. only 2 cats. have been produced: in Jan. + June. In future, sales campaigns ~~will~~ be launched 3 times a yr.

As a result of the new ~~programmes~~ programme, an ~~new~~ extra ~~dep~~ department ~~will~~ be established called 'Mail Order Sales'. An advert. will be posted on all Notice Boards inviting staff to apply for the 10 posts wh. wl. become available. These appts. wl. be made by the end of July.

The new department will ~~will~~ be housed in the area currently occupied by the A/cs. Department, wh. who ~~will~~ ~~be~~ moving to ~~their~~ its new accom. ~~which is~~ now being prepared on the second floor.

There is likely to be some incon. caused during these changes in ~~terms~~ accom. and it will ~~will~~ be necy. to rely on the co-operation of all staff to ensure bus. is carried on without ~~too much~~ interruption + difficulty for our customers.

Task 77

Suggested time allowance: 20 minutes

Our ref. RSSC/dh

Mr J R Lambet

22 Granby Road

STROOD

Kent

ME2 3EH

Take a copy & type an envelope

Dear Mr L —

PATIO DOOR - TYPE KA/639

Thank you for your letter of 7th June and for the cheque in full settlement of our Invoice No 3509. Our official rec is enclosed, as requested.

Regarding the flaw in the glass, I understand that you are not registering a complaint but will put it on record so that, should there be any problems with this sealed unit at a later date, the coy will have had prior notice. I am confident, however, that such small flaws as occur in glass of this type from time to time do not in any way weaken the pane. I wd. at some time welcome the opp. of inspecting the work; perhaps you wd. let me know when there wd. be somebody at home so that I can carry out an inspection.

Yrs. scly

RSS CLARKE

Director

SELF-CHECK

Special points

Did you type the abbreviations in full in each task? Check your work against the following:

Task 5

business	year	will
government	guarantee	received
which,	which	through
believe,	will	accounts
company		

Task 6

acknowledge	experience	sufficient
inconvenient	temporary	which
Crescent	referred	miscellaneous
		exercise

Task 7

approximately	company	shall
appointment	expenses	recommend
will	will	receipts
necessary	responsible	immediate
receive	separate	definitely
		with

Task 8

company	year	which
catalogue	advertisement	accommodation
will	which	inconvenience
years	will	accommodation
catalogues	appointments	necessary
January	will	business
and	Accounts	and

PROGRESS REPORT

Read your work carefully for typing errors. Make corrections and then pass it to someone else to check. When you get it back, fill in your progress report (see page 11).

Once you have completed Tasks 5 – 8, move on to Tasks 9 – 11.

B4 *Practice material*

You will have found from Tasks 5 – 8 that you need to be able to read and understand the sentences containing abbreviated words before you can spell them in full. Some of the abbreviations stand for

Now you need to copy drafts in handwriting or typescript which contain all of the items from the syllabus covered in Parts One and Two.

Remember

It is particularly important to ensure that you are checking your work thoroughly and that you are finding all errors and correcting them properly. Make sure that the person checking your work knows how important it is to you and points out any mistakes you may miss.

The tasks in this section are similar to the ones that will be set in the exam. They will also prepare you to work in an office. If you find that you can produce the work accurately, but have difficulty in meeting the time allowances, you should:

1   go back to the straightforward practice material in Part Three Practice Material (1) and use the exercises there to increase your typing speed;
2   re-type tasks in this section to achieve a higher production rate;
3   note the *type* of task that seems to give you the greatest difficulty – for example, if column work seems to take you a long time – and practise that sort of exercise until your rate of production improves.

Task 76

Suggested time allowance: 15 minutes

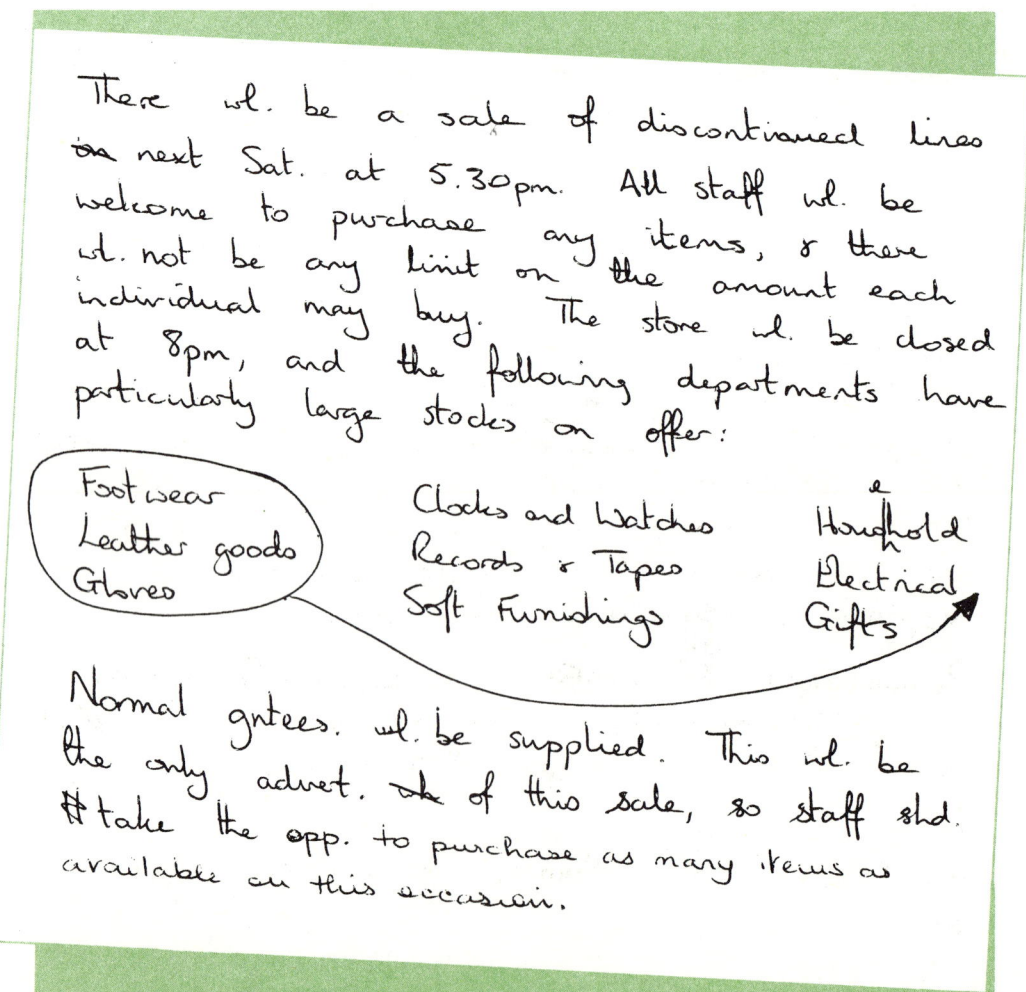

There wl. be a sale of discontinued lines on next Sat. at 5.30pm. All staff wl. be welcome to purchase any items, & there wl. not be any limit on the amount each individual may buy. The store wl. be closed at 8pm, and the following departments have particularly large stocks on offer:

Footwear
Leather goods
Gloves

Clocks and Watches
Records & Tapes
Soft Furnishings

Household
Electrical
Gifts

Normal gntees. wl. be supplied. This wl. be the only advert. of this sale, so staff shd. take the opp. to purchase as many items as available on this occasion.

different words, and it is only by thinking carefully about the meaning of each sentence that you can decide which word to use. *Remember*: if it doesn't make sense, you have chosen the wrong word.

Tasks 9 – 11 will give you further practice.

Task 9

At the cttee. meeting it was decided to dev. connections w. local mfrs. who wd. be prepared to provide epps. for^on yr. temp. employment scheme. We trust this wl. be successful, but of course we cannot gntee. that suff. firms wl. come forward to take up all of yr. employees. The sec. has ~~had~~ already recd. a list of sigs. from ~~interested~~ people who attended the cttee. meeting and ~~could~~ wish to join the scheme.

Task 10

The holiday in Section Two of our cat. ^catalogue wl. cause you greater exp.^experience but provide you with a rewarding exp. hard to forget. Just put yr. sign^signature to the booking form & you will rec. tickets for the best opp.^opportunity of yr. yr. — a 2-month trip you will remember for the next 10 months! ✓ Only (Available) from Feb. to Apr., so don't waste time.

Task 11

Dr. Mrs Jones

We are not quite sure what you mean in yr. letter of yesterday when you (ref.^make to items in our cat. wh. are not available in small sizes. The cat. numbers you give are for furniture and bedding, + we do not bel. you intend to suggest these shd. be supplied in 25 cm and 30 cm, etc.

Perhaps you ~~will~~ will write to us again and give us appropriate details, ie page number, item description, code and price. Eg: page 592; Jumper; A4068; £5.95

We hope we ~~will~~ shall then be able to assist you further.

Yrs. scly.

Task 75 – copying typescript with amendments

Suggested time allowance: 25 minutes

FAMILY SAGAS

Look for them on

If you enjoy books based on the lives of individuals in generations of families, try these books listed below. ~~Try~~ the shelves where books are stored alpha~~be~~tically by ~~t~~he author's name.

TITLE	AUTHOR	FAMILY
Next of Kin	Gladys Hasty CARROLL	The Sturtevant family in Maine. Many lives are affected by the advent of new blood.
The Dunne Family	James T FARRELL	Irish immigrants and strangers in a new land. *in America*
Fairytales	Centhia FREEMAN	An Italian-American family which continues for generations.
The Prescott Chronicles	Albert FRIED	An American family developing from ~~earliest~~ colonial days to the present.
Sons	Evan HUNTER	The men of 3 American generations going to war.
The Young Matriarch	G B Stern *caps*	The Rakonitz family who cannot do without a Matriarch.

List compiled by Margaret Allen

Broome Stages   Clemence DANE   The Broome family who dominate English theatre from George I to the present.

SELF-CHECK

Special points

Task 9

committee	your	your
develop	temporary	secretary
with	will	received
manufacturers	guarantee	signatures
would	sufficient	committee
opportunities	will	

Task 10

catalogue	signature	your
will	and	year
expense	receive	February
experience	opportunity	April
your		

Task 11

Dear	which	believe
your	catalogue	should
reference	and	Yours sincerely
catalogue		

The abbreviations that should *not* have been typed in full are: cm, etc, ie and Eg.

PROGRESS REPORT

Read your work carefully for typing errors. Make corrections and then pass it to someone else to check. When you get it back fill in your progress report (see page 11).

Suggested time allowance: 15 minutes

CAPS / Seven Elms District – Social Workers
Estimated Cost of Visits made in 1983

	Within 3 miles £	3-5 miles £	5-10 miles £
CAPS Necessary (or) considered advisable	5,000	3,550	3,000
'No answer' calls	500	400	550
	£5,500	£4,100	£3,400

TOTAL – £13,000

Indent 15 spaces from 'No' above

'Special marks' call for special attention to be given to documents and envelopes by those sending or receiving them:

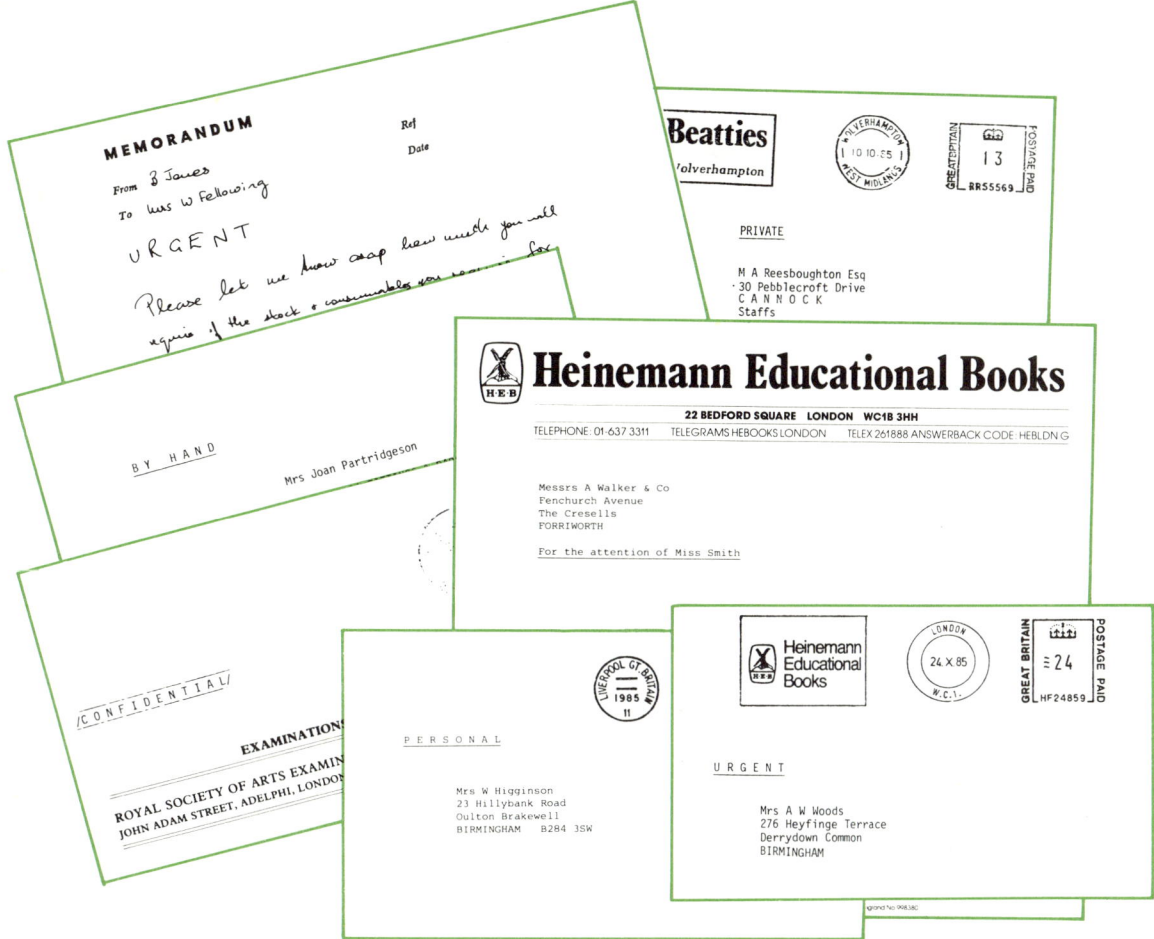

Special marks must be given some form of emphasis, for example, words shown in capitals or underlined.

They should appear at the *top* of a document that requires special attention. Such marks as 'Confidential' and 'Private' are wasted at the bottom of a document because anyone not intended to read the contents will have done so by the time they see the mark! Make sure there is at least one clear line space above and below any mark you are asked to type – just like any other heading or separate item – so that it can be clearly seen.

When working as a typist you will be expected to judge for yourself when to include special marks on *envelopes* or to use an envelope if, for example, a memo is marked 'Confidential'. You may not always prepare envelopes for memos, but you will need to do so to prevent confidential or personal information being read while being delivered!

Envelopes going through the post will be stamped or franked, and if your special mark is typed too near the top it will be covered by the cancelling marks, which normally take up about 25 – 30 mm.

If you choose to type a special mark at the bottom of an envelope, make sure you place it well to the left so that it can be seen quite apart from the address.

Task 73 – copying handwriting with abbreviations and spellings

Suggested time allowance: 20 minutes

STAFF GOLFING CLUB

There wl. be a meeting of the Cttee. on Wed. 19 March 1986 in the Staff Restaurant at 5.45 pm.

AGENDA

1. Apologies

2. Minutes

3. Matters Arising

(Inset 10 spaces from "Matters")

6.2.1. It has proved necy. to limit access to the rear cloakroom from the garden. Considerable incon. was being caused to members.

4. Shop Stocks

(Inset as above)

To consider quotations recd. with a view to ensuring suff. stocks thro' the summer.

5. Social Cttee.

(as above)

To rec. report on misc. items proposed for summer activities; to determine allowances for exps. and main purchases

6 Any Other Bus.

James Bollingay
SECRETARY

There will be *one* special mark required in every exam paper at Stage I.

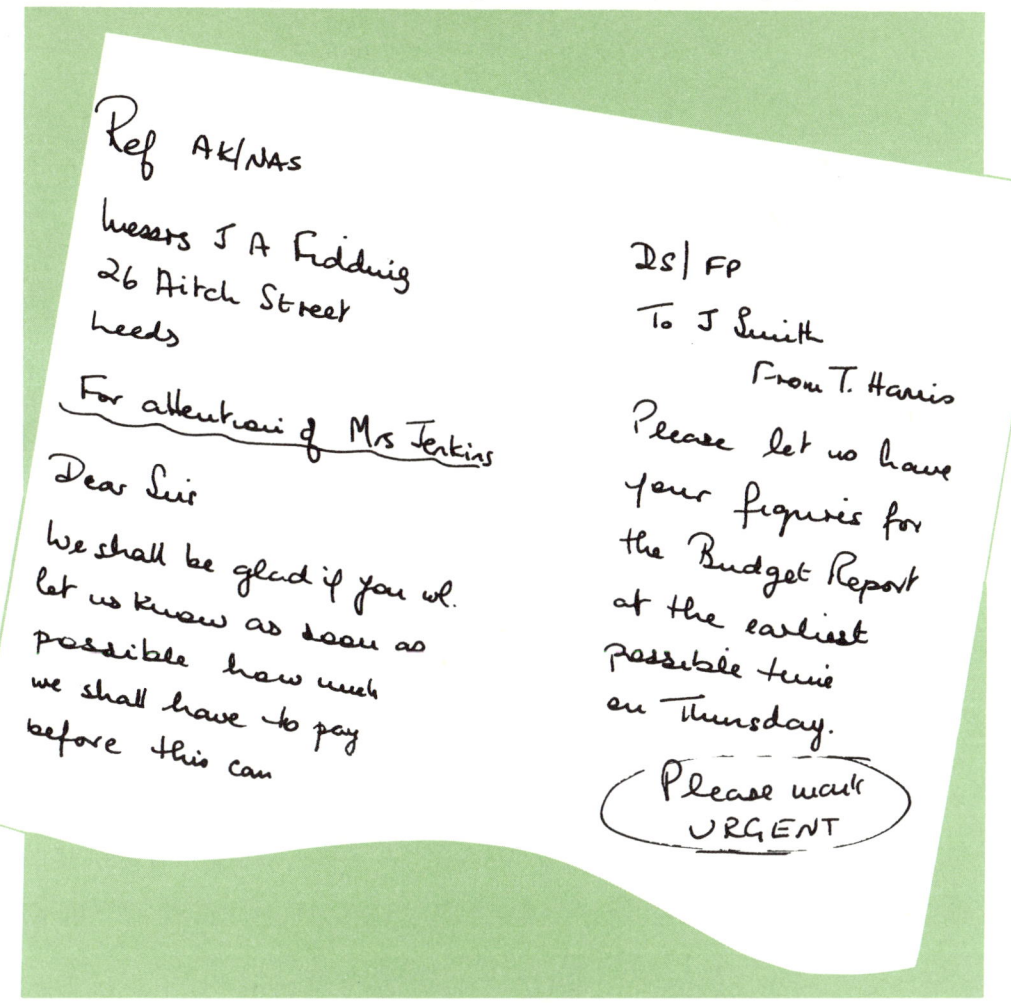

You will *not* be required to insert special marks except as instructed in the draft, that is, a mark written for you to copy or a circled instruction, as above.

Remember

If a letter includes a special mark, this should also be typed on any accompanying envelope.

WHAT THE EXAMINER WILL LOOK FOR

Accuracy

! special mark not copied
! special mark not included on any accompanying envelope
! special mark not in capitals and/or underlined as shown in the draft

Presentation

√ special mark shown as a separate item – at least one clear line space above and below.

Task 72 – copying handwriting with amendments and spellings

Suggested time allowance: 10 minutes

A group of approx. 20 elderly people in the Wilmington area recently attended the Brandon School for a Art classes.

The initiative came from the Voluntary Service Unit. Members were taken to the school by volunteer drivers and each session began with tea and cakes.

A few sixth-year girls helped to entertain the visitors.

These interested folk worked hard, with great dedication; they brought in "homework" and all said that they had immensely enjoyed the course.

In the next session, additional facilities will be available to increase the scope of the course, particularly to include some bus. topics. Watch for the adverts. wh. wl. be in the local press.

It is accepted business practice to use an enclosure mark to remind the person putting the letter into the post, or getting a memo ready for internal mail, that an item is to be included.

The mark is also important for the person receiving the letter or memo, who can then see on opening the envelope that there should be an enclosure, check whether it is there and, if not, take appropriate action to find out what has happened to it.

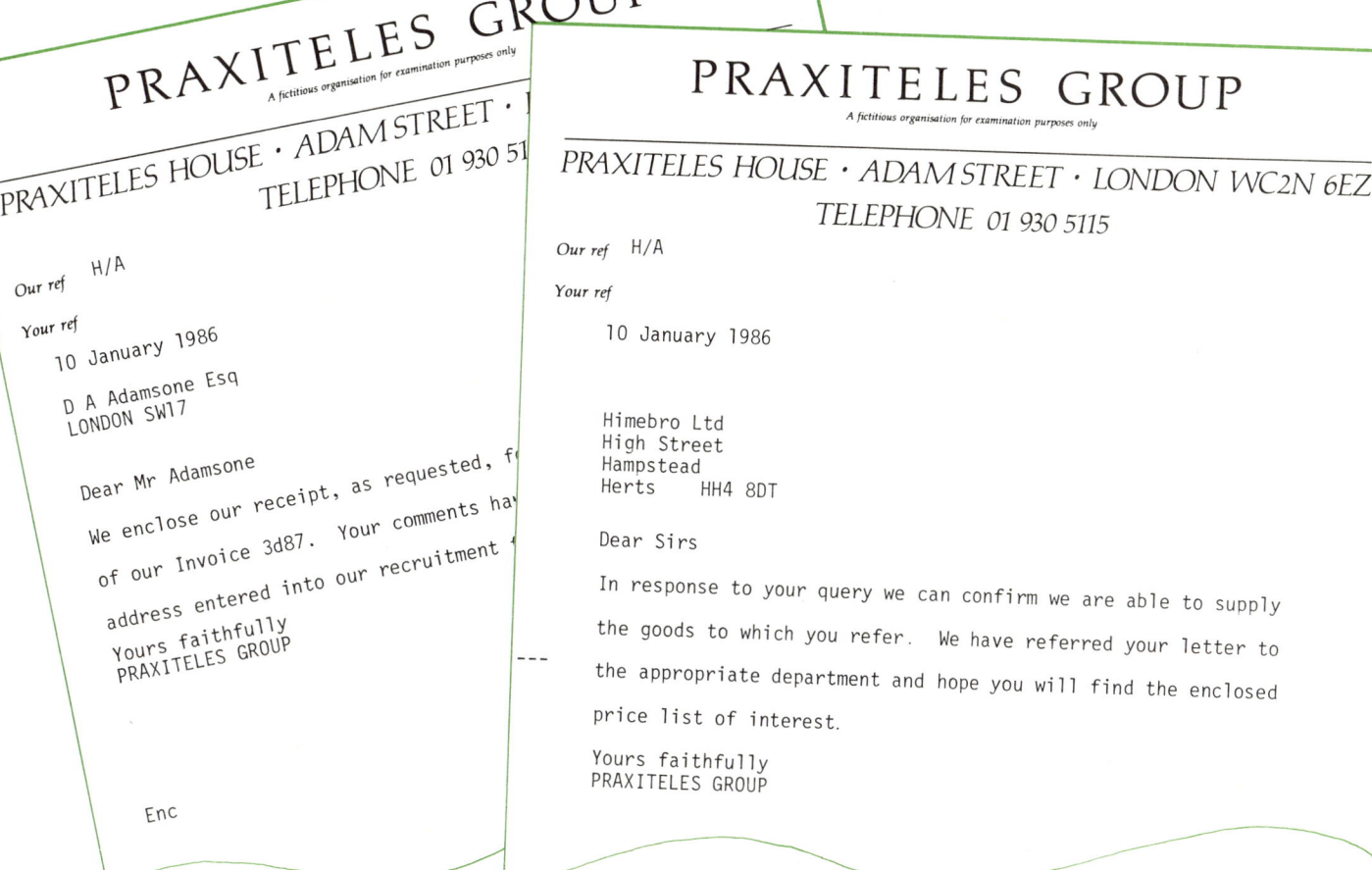

Most people seem to prefer to type 'Enc' at the end of a letter or memo – as in the example above. If you prefer this way, make a note at the bottom of the draft as soon as you notice the need for an enclosure mark – so that you do not forget to type it in.

You may prefer to type a mark in the margin on the line in which the enclosure is mentioned, as in the example above. This does, of course, save any risk of forgetting it later. Such a marginal note can be made using, for example, dots (...), dashes(---), or strokes (///) (less than three may not be noticed). Just make sure you leave room for at least one space after the mark, so that it is clearly seen and not confused with the first word of the line.

Once you are working as a typist no one will tell you when to type an enclosure mark. Your boss will expect you to notice when the wording of a letter or memo mentions an item that is to be enclosed or attached.

You should get into the habit of checking the wording of all letters and memos for the phrases: 'We enclose...' or 'the enclosed' and 'we attach...' or 'the attached'.

Task 70 – copying typescript with amendments and abbreviations

Suggested time allowance: 25 minutes

INTER-OFFICE
TIME DIFFERENCES AROUND THE WORLD

	GMT	BST
Australia	+ 10 hrs	+ 9 hrs
Brazil	− 3 hrs	− 4 hrs
Canada: West	− 8 hrs	− 9 hrs
East	− 5 hrs	− 6 hrs
Europe	+ 1 hr	Nil
~~Hong Kong~~	~~+ 8 hrs~~	~~+ 7 hrs~~
India	+ $5\frac{1}{2}$ hrs	+ $4\frac{1}{2}$ hrs
Japan	+ 9 hrs	+ 8 hrs
Malaysia	+ 8 hrs	+ 7 hrs

Task 71 – copying typescript with amendments and abbreviations

Suggested time allowance: 15 minutes

GERMAN WINES – (spaced caps)

Germany is divided into 11 wine-growing areas. The majority of
wine is white but approximately 15% of the wine produced in the
Ahr district is red. German wines should be drunk relatively
young and are best when served chilled at 53 ^{o}F (12 ^{o}C).

(Leave 6 clear line spaces)

Modern technology has come to the vineyards of the world just as
to the agricultural industry in general. Infections which attack
the vines can be treated and largely prevented by the use of
chemical sprays, which are often "delivered" by helicopters or
light planes fitted with large tanks from which the fine spray of
insecticides showers down.

One task will require an enclosure mark. Only one enclosure will be implied in the wording, and no mark will be shown in the draft for you to copy.

The mark is equally acceptable as 'Enc' at the foot of the document *or* a group of typed dots/dashes/strokes in the margin on the line where the enclosure is mentioned.

Remember

It is easy to forget to type the mark, even though you have noticed the need for one. As a reminder for yourself, write it on the exam paper as soon as you see which task requires an enclosure mark.

WHAT THE EXAMINER WILL LOOK FOR

Accuracy

! omission of an enclosure mark when required
! addition of an enclosure mark when not required

Presentation

√ at least one clear line space above 'Enc' at foot of document
or
√ at least one clear space after mark in the margin

LEISURE BANK

With effect from 1 Oct. 1986 a leisure bank will be available to professional staff. This will allow overtime in excess of one hour per day to be stored up (rather than paid) at the employer's discretion in the winter and taken, at the senior manager's discretion, as extra holiday in the summer.

For the first year the scheme will be on a trial basis. The detailed rules, which will be incorporated in the next edition of the staff handbook, include the following main points:-

Paragraph 76

The Scheme is only available to professional staff who are paid for overtime.

Paragraph 77

At the option of the employee, during the months of Oct.-April, overtime in excess of an average of one hour per day of time worked in a month can be carried forward.

Paragraph 80

It may be redeemed at the rate of one hour's holiday for one hour's overtime, at any time from May-Sept. but only with the agreement of the departmental manager.

Paragraph 81

Any time carried forward but not taken at 30 Sept. each year will be paid as overtime with the salary from Oct.

STUDENTS STUDYING

This scheme will supersede the arrangements in force which allow students to take overtime as study leave. On the basis that redemption of time will be for additional studying, students may redeem time at any stage during the year but only with the agreement of the departmental manager. Similarly, they may add time to the leisure bank at any time during the year.

As a typist you will need to know the 'system' in your office – whether you type envelopes or it is someone else's job to do so. Then you will be expected to follow the laid-down procedure and any 'house' style for typing addresses.

The important thing is: *there must be an envelope of the right size with the right address on it.*

Always double-check! It is best to make sure of the required details from the file or your instructions, rather than following your own typing on the letter – because if you did make a mistake on the letter, it would be repeated on the envelope.

Don't let your mind wander! If there is more than one address typed in the letter (for example, in a heading) make sure you transfer the right one.

It is important that the envelope arrives at its destination with as little delay as possible. Your contribution to this is to set out the complete address clearly for sorting purposes.

Watch the following points:

1   Leave at least 25 mm clear at the top of envelopes going through the post – otherwise the address will be obscured by the postmark (see also B5 on page 31).

2   Avoid ghosting, that is, dirty marks from the ribbon because the envelope is thicker than a sheet of paper and does not curve round the roller so easily. The paper bail with its rollers pushed close together over the printing point will help you – and make sure the card holder is in place.

3   Check the bottom edge of small items such as envelopes – you may have to give added help to the machine by holding the envelope in place while you type the last line with one finger of the other hand! Otherwise your last line may be crooked or even disappear.

4   Because of the above point, don't type addresses in double-line spacing, unless the envelope is really large and you have plenty of space.

5   Type the address with the longer edge of the envelope at the top. There is no rule about this, but it is more usual, except with the very large narrow envelope – and the unusual may cause delay in sorting.

6   Some people prefer to type the postal town in capital letters as an aid to mail sorting. This is not essential, particularly as much post office sorting is now based on postcodes, but it is acceptable and you may like to add this refinement to your work – just be sure that you highlight the *town* if you are trying to help the sorter (to highlight the local suburb, or the county may be unhelpful).

If you prefer to use 'indented' style, it is important to inset each line the *same number of spaces*.

```
Messrs James & Holden
      212-228 Verricon Street
         Purcival Berriman Common
            Mainwaring
               PLYMOUTH  PB8 4T2
```

The tasks in this section cover syllabus items B3 – B4 and C1 – C12.

You may find that you are not able to type accurately the items in this section within the times suggested, until you have practised some of the material in earlier chapters.

Now you need to copy work in handwriting or typescript that contains:

1   amendments to the text;
2   abbreviated words that you must spell in full;
3   abbreviations that you must not spell out.

You should watch carefully for instructions to:

1   leave spaces;
2   use capitals;
3   inset from the left-hand margin;
4   use a specific line spacing.

Task 68 – copying handwriting with amendments and abbreviations
(see B3 and B4 on pages 18 – 30).

Suggested time allowance: 20 minutes

PRAXIBOWL

How to score

1. Each game consists of 10 frames.
2. There are 10 pins to knock down in each frame.
3. You bowl 2 balls in each frame, unless your first is a "strike" – all pins down with 1 ball.
4. If you get all pins down with two balls this is called a "spare".
6. If you don't get all ten pins down with 2 balls you just score the number you knocked down.
8. A "strike" scores 10 plus the pins you get with your next 2 balls.
9. A "spare" scores 10 plus the pins you get with your next ball.
10. The score is totalled progressively from frame to frame.
If you get a "strike" in the tenth frame you are entitled to 2 bonus balls.
7. If you get a "spare" in the tenth frame you are entitled to 1 bonus ball.

IN THE EXAM

One envelope will be requested – *and only one envelope will be supplied in the stationery pack.*

The envelope may not be required for the letter. There are no rigid requirements regarding how or where to type the address, but it must be accurate.

It is not essential to adopt the same style as you have used for the address on a letter or other relevant document – but you may feel to do this would add refinement to your work.

Remember

Any special mark on a document must be typed on an envelope enclosing that document (see B5 Special Marks on page 31).

(see B5 Special Marks on page 31)

WHAT THE EXAMINER WILL LOOK FOR

- Failure to type the envelope may mean that you have not completed the exam and cannot pass.

Accuracy

! errors or omissions in names and addresses
! omission of special marks when applicable

Presentation

√ address clear and sensibly placed
√ no 'ghosting' or crooked lines

Note:
The envelope supplied by the RSA for use in the examination is DL size (220 × 111 mm).

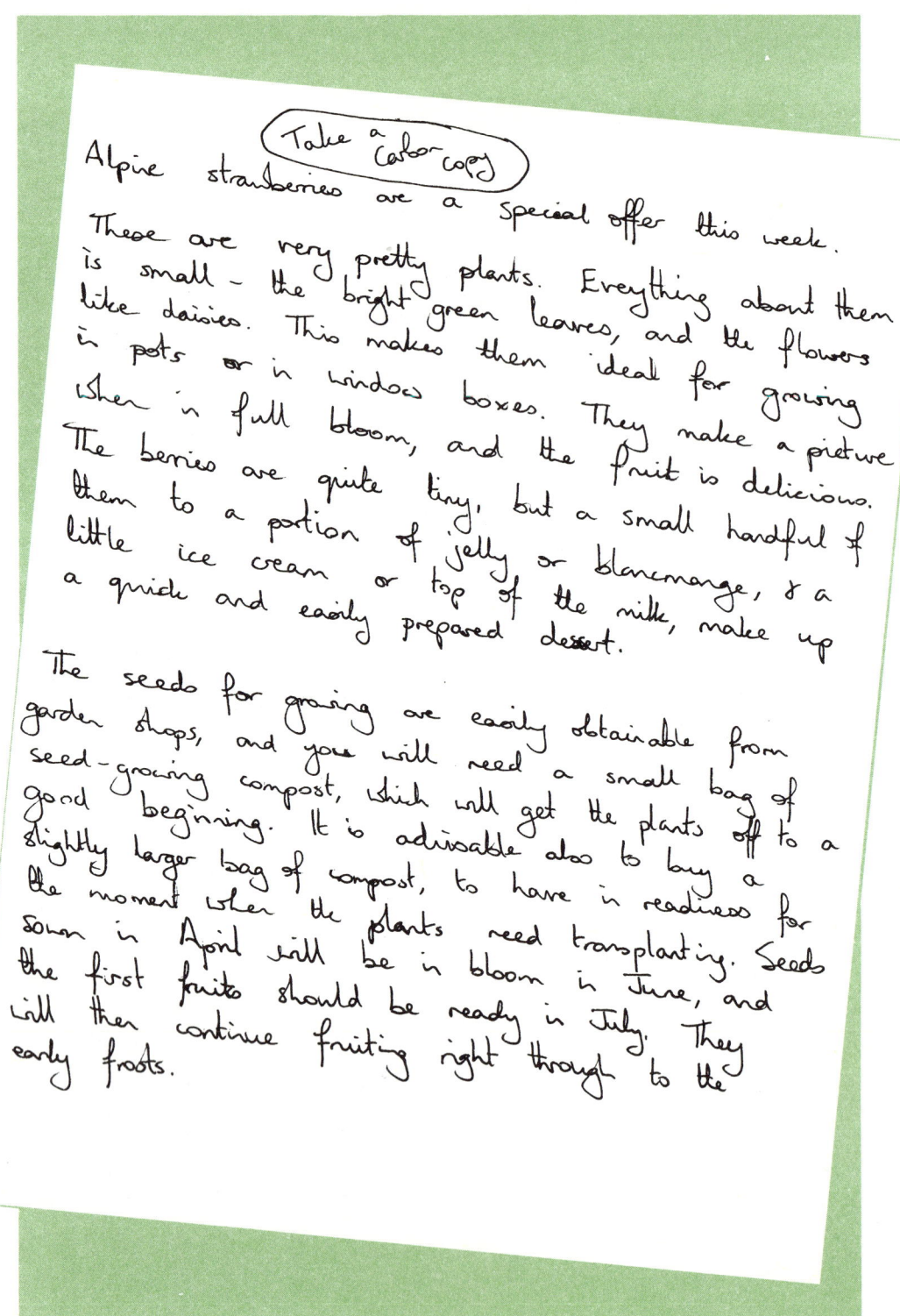

Take a
(Carbon copy)

Alpine strawberries are a special offer this week. These are very pretty plants. Everything about them is small - the bright green leaves, and the flowers like daisies. This makes them ideal for growing in pots or in window boxes. They make a picture when in full bloom, and the fruit is delicious. The berries are quite tiny, but a small handful of them to a portion of jelly or blancmange, & a little ice cream or top of the milk, make up a quick and easily prepared dessert.

The seeds for growing are easily obtainable from garden shops, and you will need a small bag of seed-growing compost, which will get the plants off to a good beginning. It is advisable also to buy a slightly larger bag of compost, to have in readiness for the moment when the plants need transplanting. Seeds sown in April will be in bloom in June, and the first fruits should be ready in July. They will then continue fruiting right through to the early frosts.

The following practice tasks include all of the items so far dealt with in Part One. They are two personal business letters for Miss Jenny Markham and a note of a telephone conversation.

Type all three tasks and complete the self-check before passing your work to someone else to read.

Task 12

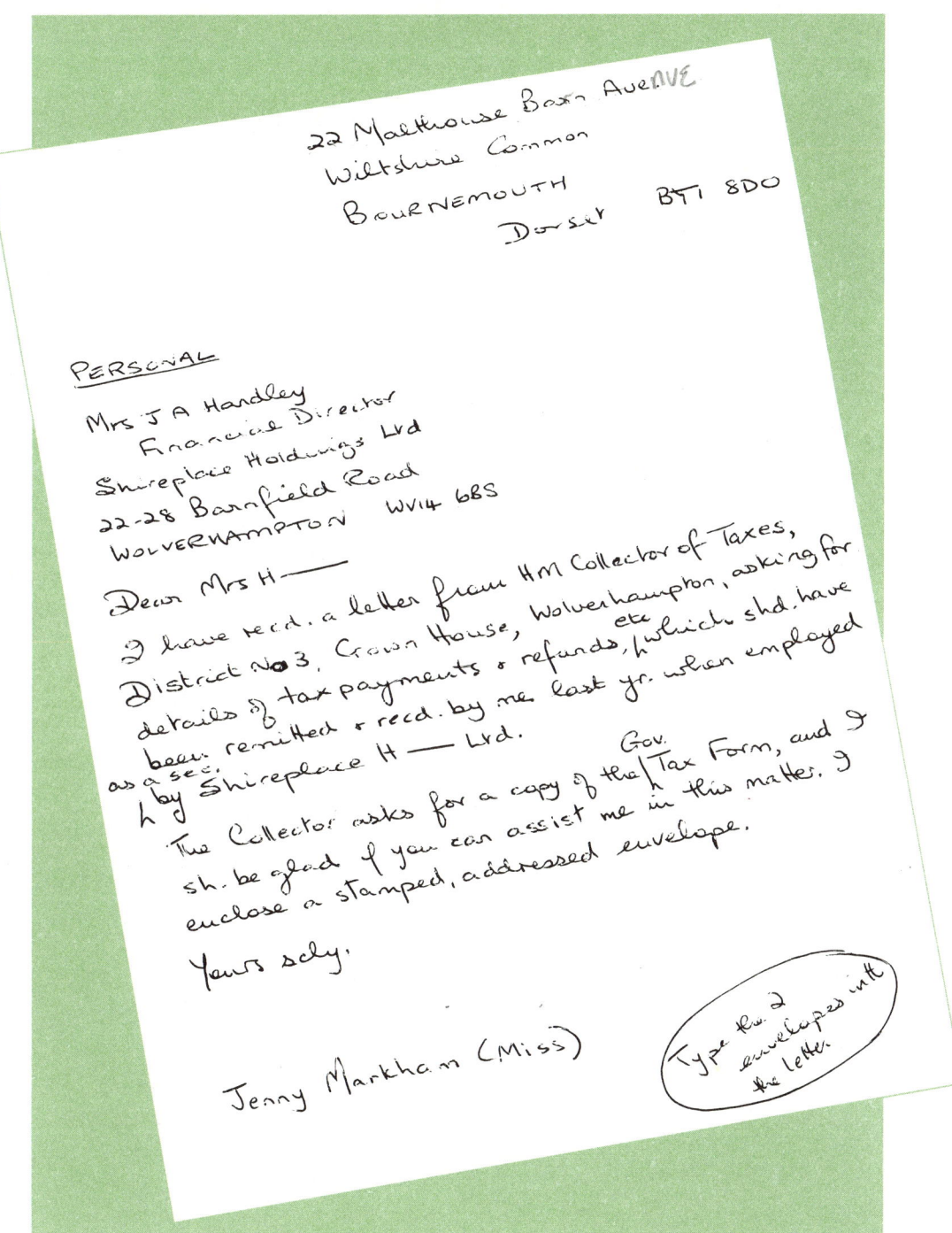

22 Malthouse Barn Avenue
Wiltshire Common
BOURNEMOUTH
Dorset   BT1 8DO

PERSONAL

Mrs J A Handley
   Financial Director
Shireplace Holdings Ltd
22-28 Barnfield Road
WOLVERHAMPTON   WV14 6BS

Dear Mrs H——

I have recd. a letter from HM Collector of Taxes, District No 3, Crown House, Wolverhampton, asking for details of tax payments & refunds, etc, which shd. have been remitted & recd. by me last yr. when employed as a sec. by Shireplace H—— Ltd.

The Collector asks for a copy of the Gov. Tax Form, and I sh. be glad if you can assist me in this matter. I enclose a stamped, addressed envelope.

Yours sdcly.

Jenny Markham (Miss)

Type the 2 envelopes with the letter.

Task 65 – copying handwriting without amendments

Suggested time allowance: 9 minutes

The system for ordering and re-ordering stocks of consumable items will be changed next month. All those concerned should obtain detailed instructions from their Supervisors, who will have been notified of the new procedures and be in possession of new stationery to be used.

This reorganisation has been agreed at all levels and for all departments. No stationery ordered by previous methods will be forthcoming and it is imperative that all personnel review their current stocks and needs for the immediate future in time to allow for any delays which may initially occur upon implementation of the new system.

Task 66 – copying handwriting without amendments

Suggested time allowance: 6 minutes

TO STORE YOUR VIDEO CASSETTES

Always put the cassette back in its case before storage. Store in a vertical position.

Keep in a cool and dry place and avoid storing in direct sunlight or near sources of heat. Do not drop or otherwise subject the cassette to shock impact.

For best results store the cassette with the tape fully rewound.

If the tape has been rewound unevenly, rewind it once again to "pack" the tape properly.

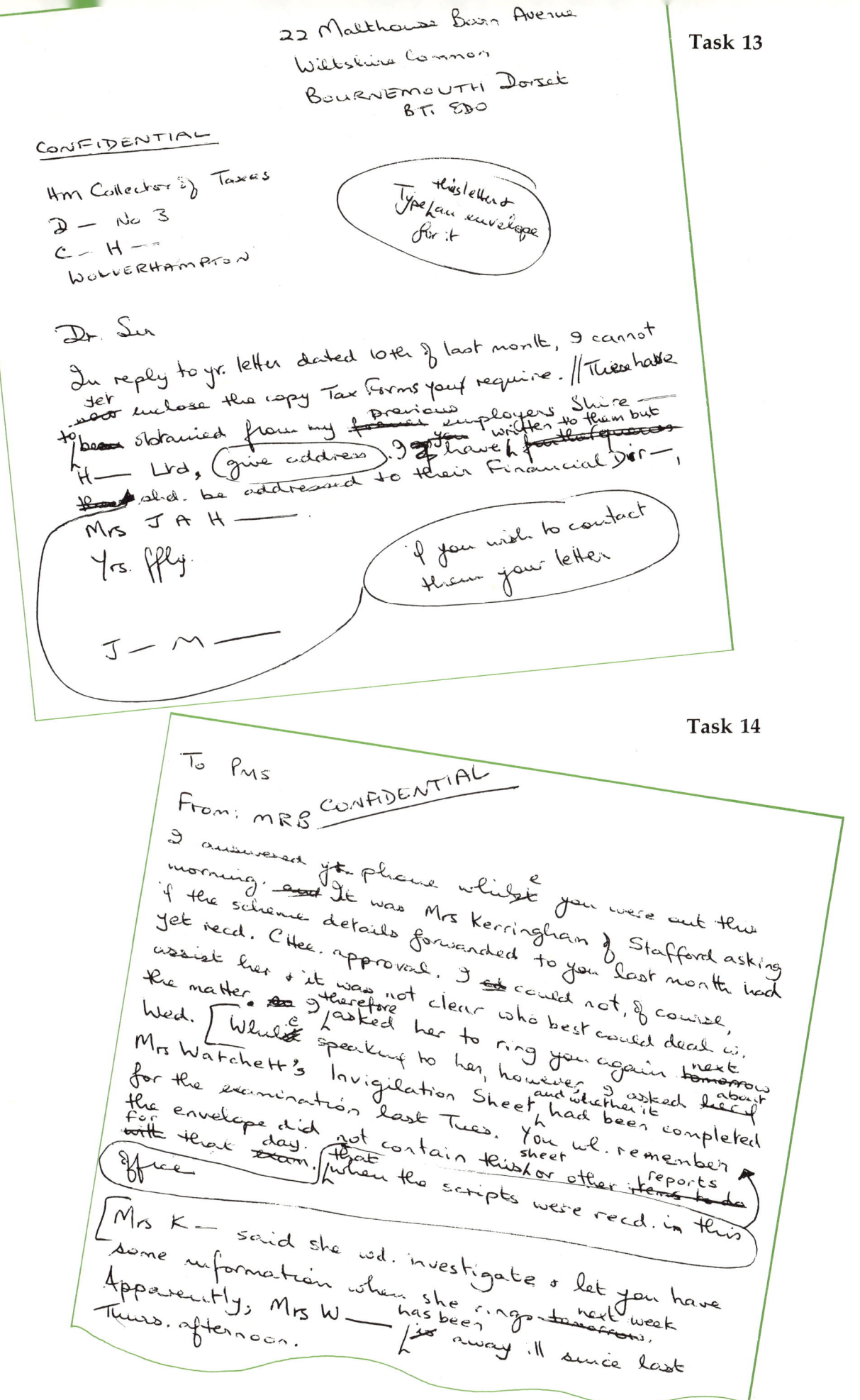

22 Malthouse Barn Avenue
Wiltshire Common
BOURNEMOUTH Dorset
BT₁ 8DO

CONFIDENTIAL

Hm Collector of Taxes
D — No 3
C — H —
WOLVERHAMPTON

Type this letter & an envelope for it

Dr Sir

In reply to yr. letter dated 10th of last month, I cannot yet enclose the copy Tax Forms you require. // These have to been obtained from my previous employers Shire — H — Ltd, (give address). I have written to them but shd. be addressed to their Financial Dir —,

If you wish to contact them your letter

Mrs J A H —

Yrs. ffly.

J — M —

To PMS

From: MRB   CONFIDENTIAL

I answered yr phone whilst you were out this morning. It was Mrs Kerringham of Stafford asking if the scheme details forwarded to you last month had yet recd. Cttee. approval. I could not, of course, assist her & it was not clear who best could deal w. the matter. I therefore asked her to ring you again next [tomorrow] speaking to her, however, I asked her about and whether it Invigilation Sheet had been completed for the examination last Tues. You wl. remember the envelope did not contain this or other items when the scripts were recd. in this office

Mrs Watchett's

Mrs K — said she wd. investigate & let you have some information when she rings next week Apparently, Mrs W — has been away ill since last Thurs. afternoon.

Contrary to popular belief, most burglaries take place during the day. The quick dash you make to the shops before they close, or to collect the children from school, presents ideal opportunities. The tell-tale garage door left open because you did not have time to slam it shut before you rushed away, is as good as an invitation.

About a third of the illegal entries are through the front of the house, and in many of these cases it is simply a matter of pushing the front door open. Other entries are through the back, where a ventilator open or a window not fully closed is a nice welcoming sign. It is a sobering thought that if you have not been burgled so far, it is probably not because your house is too difficult to get into, but because the burglary profession is seriously undermanned, and there are not enough thieves to go round.

Your best protection is to make sure that it is not worth the risk of breaking in, that is, your precautions have to be good enough to put anybody off. The first step to better security is to convince yourself that your house really could be entered unlawfully, and that it would be pretty unpleasant. The shock of finding your home ransacked is at least as painful as the actual financial losses suffered. You need to take notice of the anti-theft campaigns mounted by the police from time to time.

SELF-CHECK

Special points

Task 12

Did you

1 date the letter accurately?
2 include the special mark, PERSONAL?
3 complete the gaps with Handley and Holdings?
4 type Enc at the bottom of the letter – or insert a mark in the margin on the relevant line?
5 spell in full the following: Avenue, received, should, and, received, year, secretary, Government, shall, Yours sincerely?
6 keep the abbreviations: Ltd, HM, No 3, etc?
7 type the envelopes to:
(a) Mrs J A Handley;
(b) Miss J Markham?

```
PERSONAL                        PERSONAL

Mrs J A Handley                 Miss J Markham
    Financial Director          22 Malthouse Barn Avenue
Shireplace Holdings Ltd         Wiltshire Common
22-28 Barnfield Road            BOURNEMOUTH
WOLVERHAMPTON   WV14 6BS         Dorset    BT1 8DO
```

Task 13

Did you

1 date the letter accurately?
2 include the special mark, CONFIDENTIAL?
3 complete the gaps with: District, Crown House; Shireplace Holdings, 22 – 28 Barnfield Road, Wolverhampton WV14 6BS; Financial Director, Mrs J A Handley; Jenny Markham?
4 spell in full the abbreviations for: your, should, Yours faithfully?
5 amend the second paragraph? This should now read:

```
These have to be obtained from my previous employers,
Shireplace Holdings Ltd, 22-28 Barnfield Road,
Wolverhampton WV14 6BS.  I have written to them but
if you wish to contact them your letter should be addressed
to their Financial Director, Mrs J A Handley.
```

6 realise that no enclosure mark should be included?
7 type an envelope?

2   If you forget to take a carbon copy you have not satisfactorily completed the task in the time allowed. The rate of production includes time for interpreting instructions, as well as organising materials, for example, making up and separating carbon sets.

3   Concentration is the essence of copying skill.

Before you start to type:

(a) wipe your fingers on a tissue; flex them to feel their strength and make each finger work separately;

(b) put paper into machine, get it straight, and *check* the margins are set properly, the line-space regulator and position of shift lock;

(c) scan the material again to remind yourself of its subject;

(d) check task instructions again, making sure you understand them, writing notes if necessary.

(e) set your mind to exclude everything else but the work.

While you are typing:

(a) keep your concentration – few tasks will take as long as 30 minutes;

(b) follow the meaning of the sentences and watch out for words which at first do not seem to make sense. Check the whole sentence until the meaning is clear;

(c) correct your work as you go along. Trying to remember to go back and do it afterwards can disturb your concentration and cause you to make more errors.

After typing:

(a) check again to see if you missed any errors and make any corrections needed;

(b) now check the task instructions again, making sure you have carried them out properly.

After removing your work from the typewriter place it flat, face down, on a protective piece of paper, well away from your machine, correcting materials and carbon paper.

Task 63 – copying perfect typescript

Suggested time allowance: 8 minutes

```
If you are hanging a wallpaper that requires pasting, you will need a flat
table to work on.  A folding pasting table is ideal, or a flush door that has
had the handles and catches removed is a good substitute.  You will need sharp
shears or scissors, and a paste brush.  A paper-hanging brush is also essential,
to smooth paper down on to the wall.  You can improvise a plumb line by tying
some heavy metal nuts to the end of a length of thin string.  A seam roller is
useful for pressing the edges of paper against the wall, but should never be
used on embossed papers.

To find out how many rolls to buy, first measure the height of the walls from
skirting to ceiling, and measure the distance around the entire room.  Take
these measurements with you to the shop, and consult the rollage chart there,
which will indicate how many rolls are needed, and if you are in doubt, buy
an extra roll.  The supplier may agree to take this back afterwards, if you
find you do not need it after all.
```

Did you

1   date the note accurately?
2   include the special mark CONFIDENTIAL or <u>Confidential</u>?
3   complete the gaps with: Mrs Kerringham, Mrs Watchett?
4   spell in full the following: your; received; Committee; and; with; Wednesday; Tuesday; will; received; would; and; Thursday?
5   keep the abbreviations PMS and MRB (there is no way you can possibly know who these are)?
6   note that no enclosure mark is to be inserted?
7   type an envelope as follows?

```
     To:  PMS                         CONFIDENTIAL
                        or

     CONFIDENTIAL                     To:  PMS
```

(If you did not type 'To' on the envelope it is *not* a fault.)

Check your typed work against the following:

```
CONFIDENTIAL

To: PMS                                        (date)

I answered your phone while you were out this morning.  It
was Mrs Kerringham of Stafford asking if the scheme details
forwarded to you last month had yet received Committee
approval.  I could not, of course, assist her and it was
not clear who best could deal with the matter.  I
therefore asked her to ring you again next Wednesday.

While speaking to her, however, I asked about Mrs
Watchett's Invigilation Sheet and whether it had been
completed for the examination last Tuesday.  You will
remember that when the scripts were received in this
office the envelope did not contain this sheet or other
reports for that day.

Mrs Kerringham said she would investigate and let you have
some information when she rings next week.  Apparently,
Mrs Watchett has been away ill since last Thursday
afternoon.

                    From: MRB
```

Note:
It is not a fault if you typed the memo in double-line spacing.

PROGRESS REPORT

Read your work carefully for typing faults. Make corrections and then pass it to someone else to check. When you get it back, fill in your progress report (see page 11).

The suggested time allowance is to help you produce work that would be acceptable to any employer.

Your progress reports should be used now to enter any *excess* time that you took to complete a task – which of course, means how much time you were *short of* in the suggested time allowance. For example, if the suggested time allowance is 8 minutes and you take *10* minutes, then your *shortfall* on your production rate to be entered on your report is 2 minutes, i.e − 2.

If you produce a document accurately and well presented in less than the time allowed, you should give yourself *plus time*. For example, an 8-minute task completed in 6 minutes gives you 2 minutes plus time, i.e. + 2.

In this way, you will soon see whether your rate of production is likely to meet the requirements of the RSA Stage I exam. Any shortfall should be compensated for and cancelled out by a plus-time over the work in each of the three sections.

An example of a progress report, which you should prepare for yourself, is given below. Section 1 has been filled in to show you how to complete the form.

Practice Material Section No	Task No	Time allowed (mins)	Time taken (mins)	Shortfall	Plus-time	Running total (mins)
	63	8	6		+2	+2
	64	8	11	−3		+1
1	65	9	12	−3		−4
	66	6	5		+1	−3
	67	14	10		+4	+1
2						

Part Three   *Practice material (1)*

The tasks in this section can be used for practice from the beginning of your work with this book. They consist of straightforward material for copying.

Time allowances take account of:

1   inserting paper, including choosing and setting margins (see C9);
2   choosing and setting line spacing (see C3);
3   checking your work and making corrections.

Remember

1   You must copy accurately, paying careful attention to details:

    (a) do not add capital letters – type those in the draft;
    (b) leave at least one clear line between paragraphs;
    (c) use same spacing after punctuation throughout your work.

Sometimes a word that is clear to some (and perhaps most) people is not always clear to everyone. This may be because the word is unknown to the reader, or because of difficulty in reading the draft.

It will help you if you always copy exactly words that you do not know, but which seem to be written very clearly. Remember that foreign words may include accents and these must also be copied: this will mean inserting them in handwriting (unless you are using a keyboard which includes accents). If you have to copy words you do not know and which do not seem to be names or in a foreign language, check in a dictionary to make sure the words you have typed do exist.

It does, of course, sometimes happen that you come to a word which does not seem sensible and you may even be unable to read the first letters, so that it is impossible for you to check it in a dictionary. In this case you could try:

1   looking forwards and backwards in the document to find the same shape letter in a word that you can read (people usually write repeated words in the same way);
2   reading the whole sentence or paragraph to get the sense, which will help you identify the 'blank' word;
3   closing your eyes for a few seconds; then looking back at the offending, unfamiliar word;
4   moving to another task that requires planning or reading through before attempting to continue with the problem word(s).

IN THE EXAM

Every effort is made to ensure that the handwriting in tasks for Stage I is straightforward and clear.

Special efforts are made to present names, addresses, figures and any foreign words particularly clearly, and wherever possible to avoid technical or specialist words.

Remember

Check your copying of unfamiliar or foreign words, including names, letter by letter with the exam paper.

WHAT THE EXAMINER WILL LOOK FOR

Accuracy

!   each word not 100 per cent accurate

Developing Your Rate of Production

Section A of the Typewriting Skills syllabus requires that candidates must use their machines to work at a *rate of production* adequate to complete six business tasks (including a carbon copy and envelope) within two hours, working from handwritten and typewritten drafts.

There is no *copy typing speed test* in the RSA Stage I Typewriting Skills exam. If you wish to obtain a certificate showing the speed at which you can type perfect copy, there is an RSA test, which you can enter separately.

The production rate includes time for:

1 machine manipulation, that is, keying-in/setting margins/tabulating/etc.;
2 organising your time and your materials;
3 scanning, reading and interpreting instructions and drafts;
4 reading for the meaning of material to find information as well as to interpret handwriting;
5 use of styles and conventions, for example, letter and memo formats.

IN THE EXAM

You need to complete all of the work set in order to demonstrate that you can produce work at a rate of 450 words per hour.

PRACTICE MATERIAL

So that you can measure your own rate of production, each piece of practice material in Part Three gives a time allowance. This takes account of all of the different activities involved in typewriting – including checking your work and correcting it. Therefore, your work needs to be completed in every respect, and ready to 'hand over', within the time set.

The practice material in this part has been divided into three sections:

Section 1 contains straightforward copying exercises, and in one task, a carbon copy is required. Tasks 63 – 64 require you to copy perfect typescript, and Tasks 65 – 67 are to be copied from handwriting.

Section 2 covers syllabus items B3 – B4 (see pages 3 – 4) and C1 – C12 (see page 5). You may find that you are unable to type accurately within the times suggested the items in this section until you have practised some of the material in earlier parts.

Section 3 includes all material covered in Parts One and Two. Now you will be using all of the skills that make up competence in typewriting at this level and which you need to be able to carry out fluently and effectively.

In Part Three your progress reports will focus on the speed at which you can produce work that is both free of error and attractive in appearance. *Remember*: no matter how quickly work is produced, it is useless if inaccurate and not presented so as to be intelligible as a letter, a memo, etc.

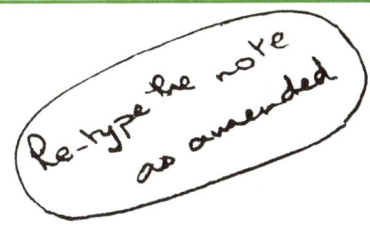
Re-type the note as amended

From: Copy Section

To: Illustrations Department

Ref: JAS/COOK

2.2.86 (today's date)

The entries to be made at p. 186 272 in the ~~BJB~~ JAS COOK REFERENCE are as follows:

~~COLD LEMON SOUFFLE~~ Cold Lemon Souffle

A light, refreshing dessert, particularly good after a heavy meal. The souffle looks most attractive if it is set in a ~~6-inch~~ 15 cm ~~souffle~~ dish, tied with a raised collar of waxed or greaseproof paper. the paper is removed When the souffle is set and the top of the souffle may then be decorated with chopped or slivered nuts, biscuits (cookies) or glace cherries and cream.

Gâteau Noisette

Layers of meringue sandwiched together with a rich chocolate buttercream and covered with hazel nuts. Gâteau Noisette is a superb dessert for a dinner party.

Crème Brulée

A rich, delicious dessert, with a topping of crisp caramelised brown sugar, Crème Brulée makes an impressive end to a dinner party.

Zuccotto

A well-known Italian dessert which resembles a pumpkin in shape. Serve this rich, spectacular-looking dessert at a special dinner party.

Parents feel that they are expected to end each day by leading their complaint children upstairs for a leisurely bath, followed by a peaceful bedtime story, and then they can leave them with a goodnight kiss to have sweet dreams until the next morning.

But reality is not often like that. Everyone is tired. There are toys and bits of Lego all over the place, and the kitchen are in chaos, although there is yet one more meal to be prepared in it. Tempers get frayed, and bedtime becomes a battle of wits.

The main trouble is simply a matter of timing. How would you react yourself if someone suddenly announced that it was time for everybody to go out somewhere, just when you were immersed in a book, or in the middle of some activity that was going well? The probability is that you would resent it, and yo would protest. It is the same with children. It may not appear as though they are doig anything much, but they too can be lost in their own wolr,d and if they are jolted back into the grown-up world too precipitately they do not like it. At least 5 minutes' warning should be given before the moment of bedtime. This gives time to finish what is being done. If there is agreat deal of gear to put away after playing, even this ammount of time may not be enough, so an even earlier warning needs to be given. Hlep should be given with putting everything away. Clearing up after using toys or eqipment is an important thing for chi,dren to learn in their early childhood. It is a pity that parents are often in sucha hurry that they find it earier to clear up themselves, rather than slow down to help.

Typists are sometimes asked to re-type edited documents, even though the work may have been typed the first time by someone else.

People who edit drafts do not always write in the correction that is needed; they simply show that an error has been made. As a typist you must be able to see what needs to be done to correct typographical errors. It is also possible to see how to correct obvious errors in the wording or punctuation if you read the complete sentence in order to gain understanding of the meaning. For example, 'All of these letters *has* today's date' should be typed as 'All of these letters *have* today's date', and 'What is the date' should be punctuated as 'What is the date?'

This is not as easy as it sounds, but it is part of the skill you have been gradually developing throughout Part One of this book: reading intelligently, not skipping words; 'listening' to what you read – particularly when checking your own work; making a note in your progress report of anything you do not get right first time; caring about getting it right and finding out how to improve your performance. If you pay attention to meanings and look up in a dictionary any words you do not understand – whether you have typed them accurately or made errors first time – you will soon find you are able to cope with the work you are set as a beginner-typist. *But you must care enough to bother!*

By the tiem this notice appears most staff will be aware
that there will be no possibidity of the use of thecanteen
for the staff clubs proposed series of meetings in the
summer.

It is proposed however, that the staff restroom will be

opened on each Wednesday during August for the purpose.
The meetings cannot be arranged for longer than two
hours sunless it is for company business. but if the
Secretary is prepard to confirm the purpose as recreational this accommodation can be made available 7-9 pm.

KEY:

By the time this Notice appears most staff will be aware
that there will be no possibility of the use of the
canteen for the staff club's proposed series of meetings
in the summer.

It is proposed, however, that the staff restroom will be
opened on each Wednesday during August for the purpose.
The meetings cannot be arranged for longer than two
hours unless they are for company business, but if the
Secretary is prepared to confirm the purpose as
recreational this accommodation can be made available
7-9 pm.

(Take a Carbon Copy) to raise money for the famine victims of Ethiopia

The Live Aid Campaign / is now well-known and a lot of people who do not normally regard themselves as fans of pop music joined in, at least by watching a part of the live show on TV television.

Organised by Mr Bob Geldoff, lead singer w. Boomtown Rats, the show was televised / at least in part in 95% of the countries throughout the world with a TV network.

Over £50m is promised or has by now been recd. by the Organising Cttee. who are administering the funds by personal contact with Govs. and Relief Organisations to ensure rapid & efficient use is made of the resources made available as a result of the world-wide campaign.

~~Some of the artists taking~~

The live show was co-ordinated from London & Philadelphia. Artists taking part included:

1. Status Quo
2. Who
3. Dire Straits
4. Tina Turner
5. Mick Jagger
6. David Bowie
7. (Madonna)
8. ~~The~~ Slade
9. Queen
10. Elton John
11. Kiki Dee
12. George Michael
13. Paul McCartney
14. The Thompson Twins

IN THE EXAM

In one task only, which will always be a typed document, errors will be clearly circled. There are no other deliberate mistakes for you to find in this or other tasks in the Stage I exam, so you should not alter any word that is not circled.

There are no spelling errors for you to correct in this task. Spelling is tested in the exam through the use of abbreviated words for you to type in full (see B4 on page 4). The errors included and circled for you to correct will be selected from the following categories:

1 *Obvious typographical errors*

Shown in the exam as: Indicating:

(thereis) no likelihood	no space between words
there is no (likelihood)	overtyping
(ᵂe) shall be there	bad use of shift key so that part of letter(s) missing
and there will be no one (there) to see to the matter on our behalf	irregular left-hand margin
We shall be able to contact Mr Jones when he returns on Monday, but we do not know whether he will be bringing	irregular line spacing

2 *Obvious errors of agreement*

Shown in the exam as: To be corrected to:

The matter (are) going to be reported.	The matter is going to be reported.
Items cannot be traced through our computer unless (it was) recorded less than 7 years ago.	Items cannot be traced through our computer unless they were recorded less than 7 years ago.
She (walks) down the road yesterday.	She walked down the road yesterday.
Mr Jones (replies) to their letter on 10 January last.	Mr Jones replied to their letter on 10 January last.

RSA Typewriting Skills Book One   B9 Correcting Material Containing Errors

Complete Tasks 60 – 62. Read your work carefully. If necessary, make corrections. Then pass it to your checker. When you get it back, fill in your progress report (see page 52).

Task 60

28 Withington Hall Road
Parringham

The Sec.
Parringham Working Men's Club
Parringham

Type envelope

Dear Sir

As you will be aware, my property adjoins that of P___ W___ M___ C___ along a shared fence, ~~also~~ with conifer trees planted for its full length on ~~your~~ the Club's side.

These trees are now becoming rather large, and as such are causing a restriction of light into my rear garden. I ~~int te~~ intend, therefore, to cut approximately 3 feet off the tops of these trees.

If you have any objection to this being done, please contact me within 1 week. If I do not hear from you within this time, I will assume you have no objection and will proceed with the work.

Yours ffly.

M. A. Snelgrove

3   Obvious errors in punctuation

Shown in the exam as: To be corrected to:

Do not, be there until closing time.	Do not be there until closing time.
The Secretary quoted from the rules "No person" shall be given priority".	The Secretary quoted from the rules "No person shall be given priority".
The Manager does not wish her car to be serviced until next month. when the MOT test will be due. Please arrange this.	The Manager does not wish her car to be serviced until next month when the MOT test will be due. Please arrange this.

4   Obvious errors in use of apostrophes

Shown in the exam as: To be corrected to:

This is part of the Societys' practice.	This is part of the Society's practice.
Records of work experience will be entered in each pupils file.	Records of work experience will be entered in each pupil's file.
All of our employee's are entitled to this benefit.	All of our employees are entitled to this benefit.

WHAT THE EXAMINER WILL LOOK FOR

Accuracy

! each word not 100 per cent accurate

B9   *Practice material*

Re-type Tasks 16 – 19, making corrections.

PRAXITELES GROUP

A fictitious organisation for examination purposes only

PRAXITELES HOUSE · ADAM STREET · LONDON WC2N 6EZ
TELEPHONE 01 930 5115

Our ref

Your ref

Date ....*today*.............

Mrs Joan Harries
7 Jaceys Road
FARNHAM BEYS
Essex CM18 6NS

Dear Patient

I have made an **appointment** for you to attend Dr *Laidlaw's*

out-patient clinic on *Tuesday, 14 October next* at *2 pm*

for *follow-up consultation*

You should go to the *Main Building, Clinic 5.*

If there are any problems with the appointment please phone the Appointments

Desk on Extension *3580.*

Yours sincerely

Mary Young
Sec. to Dr Laidlaw

Task 16

There are a lot of companies ~~who~~ *which*, these days, (does) not have the computer
facilities to carry out all of their own data processing, because they
prefer to use the services of a computer bureau.

A bureau can build up sufficient custom to justify the purchase of larger
and more (xpensive) machines than an individual company may be able to
install. (this), of course, enables the bureau to complete (it's) work very
quickly, as well as undertaking jobs requiring very sophisticated (program's)
and hardware.

Task 17

The electronic (typeWriter) has now taken over the (te- t) processing machine
market for work which is not best suited to word processing packages or
machines.

There is a lot of this work which (do) not warrant occupying the micro or
word processor because, (fro) instance, it is unique and will not be required
again, nor be the basis for future repetitive work. (Mny) people forget that
while the word processor can carry out more functions than a typewriter,
the (latterstill) has its place as the (betterof) the two for certain jobs.
A prime example is form-filling.

Task 18

Your Order No 6283 (is) (rec eived) in our office yesterday. The first 4 (item)
are available from stock and will be (despatches) to your warehouse (today,)
Item 5 (2 (ton's) of Gravel No 3) will be (delivery) to your Materials Yard
early next week.

We note that your Item 6 states '10 Wheelbarrows". However (we) do not stock
such items and the catalogue number you give is not one of our (reference's)
At the time of Mr Barham's visit to our office he did (mentioned) your intention
to purchase wheelbarrows and we advised him then they were not in our list.

Complete the Car Parking Permits form for me, please

My department code is D.16

I _do_ drive to work. The two cars are as follows:

    FORD ~~CORTINA~~ SIERRA
    B 628 DYL
    Sepia

    FORD ESCORT
    A 684 DUE
    Blue

    Rear — Warehouse site

Today's date

Thank You

F W WELLS

Complete the Booking Form for
        Mrs Penelope Bracey
        44 Bracken Close
        TEWKESBURY
        Worcs.
    2 places at Birmingham from Wed. to
Fri. for one caravan.
    2 Adults   3 days   £18   MR JOHN BRACEY
                                 MRS P___ B___
    Nobody else. Total £18. Cheque enclosed
for £10   Tel. no. Tewk___ 602143.
    Today's date.

When we (discussed) the matter of the new contract at our meeting tomorrow we

must, make sure Clauses 17 and 19 (does) not take up too much time.   Clause 21

is concerned with the individual office (workers) access to further training and

must, therefore be decided upon at (tomorrows) meeting.

Everything in the contract is significant in some respect, but as next week's

staff council meeting is on the subject of training it will be more than

useful to have a decision from (Officers') on (Cluase) 21.

B9 *Practice material: self-check and progress report*

SELF-CHECK

Special points

Did you make all the corrections accurately? Check them against the following:

Task 16	Task 18	Task 19
do	was	discuss
expensive	received	must make
This	items	do
its	despatched	worker's
programs	today.	must therefore
	tons	tomorrow's
Task 17	delivered	Officers
typewriter	'10 Wheelbarrows'.	Clause
text	However,	
does	references	
for	mention	
Many		
latter still		
better of		

PROGRESS REPORT

Read your work carefully for typing faults. Make corrections and then pass your work to someone else to check. When you get it back, fill in your progress report (see page 11).

Accuracy

! inaccurate, omitted or added words
! words pre-printed on the form typed again
! entries against wrong headings – one fault for each entry, e.g. address
! deletions, i.e. wrong words crossed out or no deletions made when indicated – one fault each time this occurs
! forms signed by candidate

Presentation

√ entries within one line space of pre-printed headings
√ at least one space between headings and typed words
√ entries not overtyping dotted lines, ruled boxes or column rulings
√ words deleted effectively so that there can be no doubt which words are intended to apply

C12 *Practice material*

Tasks 56 – 59 require you to type information on forms. The forms needed for these tasks can be found in the RSA stationery section of this book.

Task 56

Complete the Insurance Form with these details: ~~shown~~
~~already shown~~

Ferndale & Sheriton Ltd
Gravesend Walk
DOVER Kent
CT 26 2LD

Today's date   Policy No 21/4286983/ML
Insured — Mrs Julia Parsons Premium £28.64
Eff. Date 2 Sept. 1986   Refer to 2/4/7

Type 'x' in boxes 2 & 4 & Type 'x' in box 7
and after box type:

→ Please advise duration of other
policy ~~eff~~ referred to.

Tasks 20 – 22 will give you an opportunity to review the items covered so far. Remember to check each one carefully after you have typed it.

Task 20

<u>Notice</u>

There has been a considerable increase in the number of ~~staff~~ members of ~~the company~~ staff cycling to work. The covered space reserved for bicycles at the end of the car park is now inadequate – bicycles left elsewhere often create/s hazards! Furthermore, there have been a few cases of (theft and damage). // To overcome these problems, the co. has converted one of the large sheds at the rear of the office block for use as a bicycle store. A new concrete floor has been laid, and there are suff. stands to accom. all staff bicycles. The spaces on the stands are numbered. The door has a security lock wh. can be opened from inside or outside, with a key (only). // Every cyclist wl. be provided with a key stamped w. the number of the space wh. has been allocated to him/her. Staff must dismount on the roadway and <u>wheel</u> their bicycles along the path & inside the store. // The Store is ready for use now. Keys can be collected from my office on production of co. identity cards.

(Today's date)

To: A/cs.
Our ref. SW1T/BA.106
From Sales Invoicing

MEMORANDUM

From Sales Invoicing   *Ref* SW1T/BA.106

To   Accounts   *Date* .. .. (today's date)

To Jenny Purton   From Amy Fellowes

MEMORANDUM

From Amy Fellowes   *Ref*

To   Jenny Purton   *Date* .. .. (today's date)

Ref IT/im2/JA139
Barry Jenkins to A D Howe
Derby Site

MEMORANDUM

From   Barry Jenkins   *Ref* IT/im2/JA139

To   A D Howe   *Date* .. .. (today's date)
     Derby Site

Only one reference will be included in memo tasks, together with names of the addressee and sender.

Note:
Since you are not asked to invent any information, nor to supply it from your own knowledge, if no courtesy titles are shown in the task (e.g. 'To John Jones' instead of 'Mr John Jones') you are not expected to add them. If you copy the draft task you will be all right!

Letter from Miss Markham (see Task 12) to Dendor Products Ltd
64 Tremlow St.
DUDLEY DY6 4EW

Dr. Sirs

Today I recd. the booklets & competition entry forms to promote your new range of 'Beauty Box' cosmetics in my shop.

Unfortunately the packages have been damaged in the post. Most of the booklets are damaged torn & dirty, the entry forms are crumpled; & none of them can be offered to customers.

I shall be glad to receive replacements but the manilla envelopes wh. you used last time were not tough enough to withstand knocks & bumps & the Post Office says these are unavoidable. I suggest you follow the advice given & use padded bags or strong cardboard boxes to send new forms & booklets.

Yours truly

J M____

Mark letter & envelope URGENT

I enclose their report &

(b) *Letterhead*

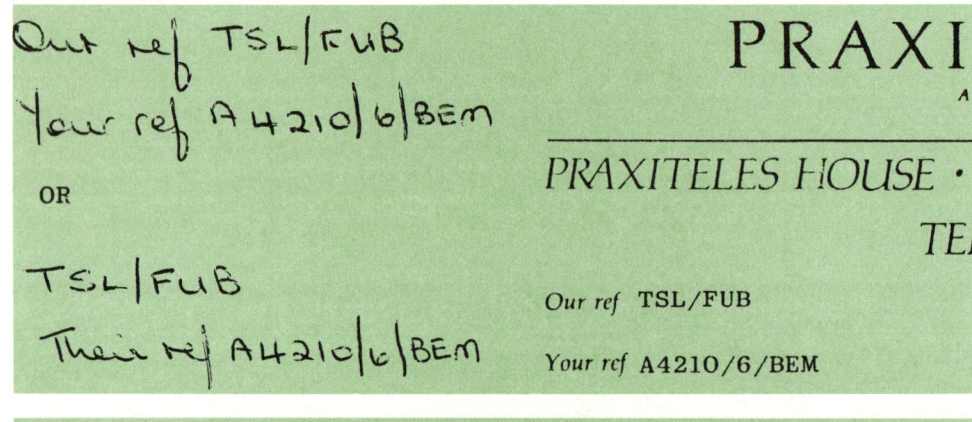

When two references are shown for a letter, they must be accurately typed in the right order. If only one reference is shown in the task, with or without the words 'Ref' or 'Our ref', it should be assumed to be the sender's reference.

(c) *Memo form*

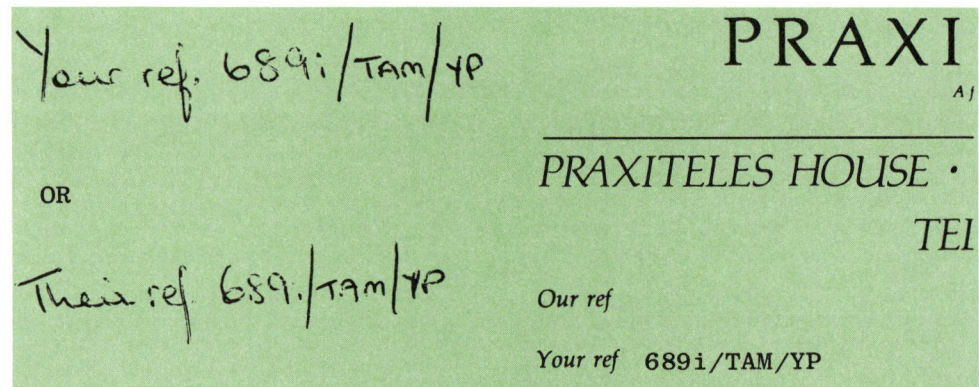

At this time of year many British families start thinking about the possibility of buying a villa or a house for future holidays or retirement in the warmer parts of southern Europe or on the other side of the Atlantic, etc.

The selection of overseas homes now being offered for sale are larger than at any time in the past ten years and the vast majority of these are in Spian.

Among the attractions of south-eastern Spain is a very mild climate where it is possible in the winter and spring to swim in the sea in the morning and to ski in the mountains after lunch. There are still many viallages and small towns which have not yet been utterly spoilt by toursim and a peaceful stroll through the narrow streets can be enjoyed. there are excellent beaches Nearby, and Granada, with its magnificient buildings, is within easy reach.

If you are interested in browsing through a list of properties and illustrated catalogues --- PHONE US: 02579-3118779-12

PRAXITELES GROUP, LONDON - Always at your service

B1 – B9 *Practice material: self-check*

Special points

If you had difficulty completing any of the tasks, the list below will help you to decide which sections you need to read again.

Task 20 included:
(a) amendments to text (B3);
(b) instruction to date (B1);
(c) abbreviations to be spelt in full (B4).

Task 21 needed:
(a) an address from Task 21 (B2);
(b) a date (B1);
(c) to be marked URGENT (B5);
(d) an envelope (B7);
(e) abbreviations to be spelt in full (B4);
(f) an enclosure mark (B6).

Task 22 included:
(a) amendments to text (B3);
(b) foreign words (B8);
(c) abbreviations (B4);
(d) circled errors (B9).

In addition to the form with dotted lines and boxes, the technique of entering the information against pre-printed headings will be tested in the examination in:

1 letters, where reference(s) should be aligned with heading(s);
2 memoranda, which include address details, date and reference headings.

Remember

You are the typist, and will *never* be asked in the exam to complete a form on your own behalf. Therefore, *do not sign the form*.

Example exam tasks

(a) *Form*

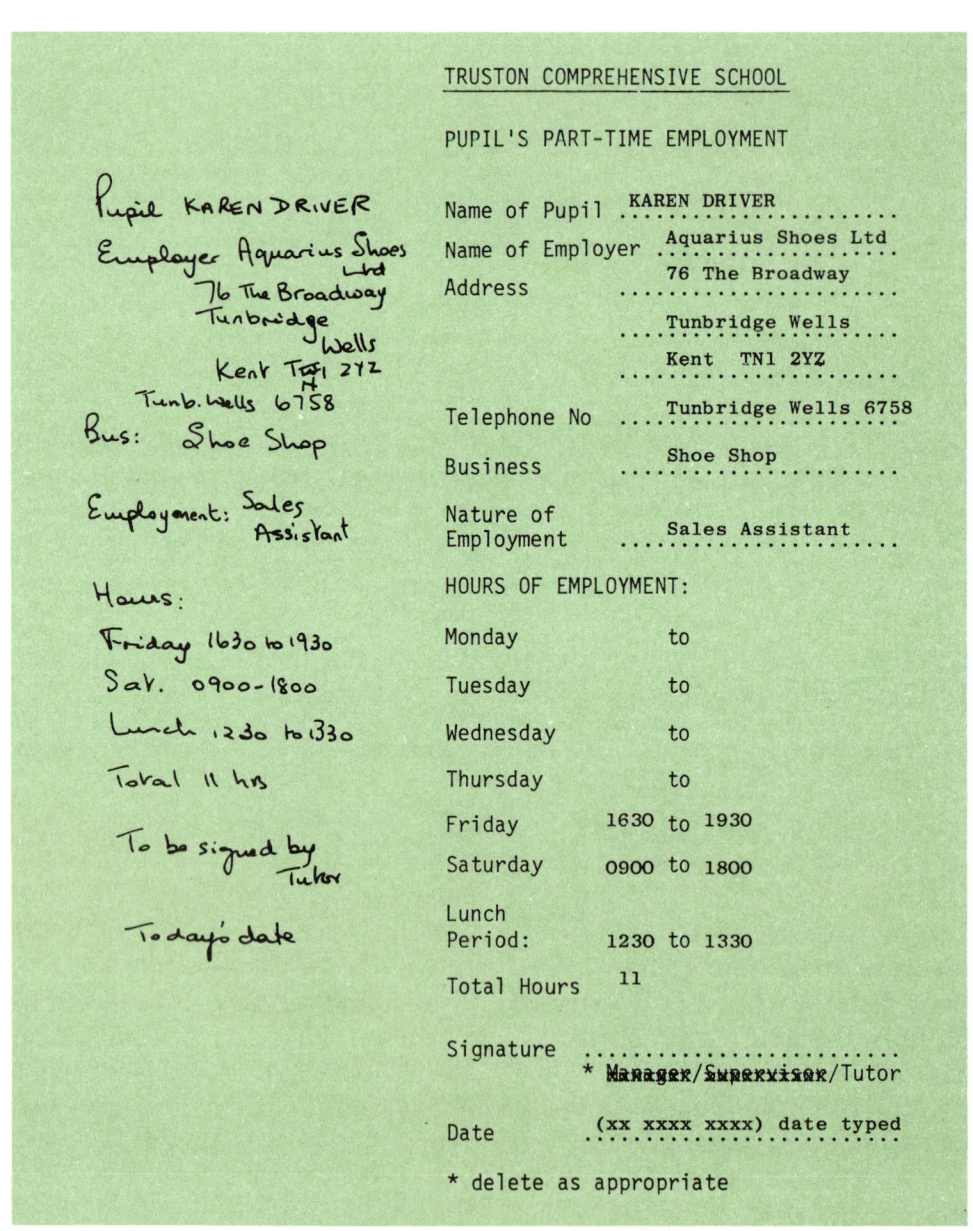

(A blank form is provided in the RSA stationery section of this book for you to practise typing the information on the above form.)

Presentation Skills

Introduction

Section C of the syllabus requires that 'candidates must use their machines to produce work which, after application of appropriate correction techniques/materials, is effectively presented and in line with current styles and conventions – including compliance with explicit and implicit instructions about presentation'. They must fulfil the objectives with no more than nine presentation faults.

Items C1 – C12 (see page 5) list the objectives explaining what sort of presentation is required and faults the examiner will be looking for. These objectives can be applied to *any* document that you may type once you are working in an office. A company may have its own 'house style' for the presentation of its correspondence or other work, and the syllabus is intended to allow anyone in the habit of using specific formats to continue to do so in the exam.

PRACTICE MATERIAL

The practice material in Part Two represents the kind of work that a typist in a first job may be expected to do. The material is not tied to any one business context except that the name of a fictitious organisation, 'Praxiteles Group', is used, in order to allow you to practise on printed stationery. This stationery is the same as that provided in the Stage I RSA exam in Typewriting Skills, and can be found at the back of this book.

The practice material is now divided into three sections, each of which brings together the work done so far in Parts One and Two. In addition, there is practice material after some of the specified items to help you to make sure that you understand the item you were covering. You do not need to have these tasks checked by someone else. They are mainly to give you the chance to decide whether you need further practice.

MAKING SURE YOU ARE CHECKING YOUR WORK
PROPERLY

Your diary system is now extended. You should continue to check your progress by filling in a report after you have completed each section. You now need to ask the person who checks your work to sign your progress report *only* if they would be prepared to send out your typing as real work - that is, work well presented and free from fault. The responsibility of signing your report may make sure your checker takes particular care. Some people may find it easier (and kinder) to write and list faults rather than to tell you face-to-face. (You will now be asking for packages of work, not single tasks, to be checked. It may be easier if you can leave your work and progress report with your checker for comment, for you to collect later.)

Typing on Forms

Filling in forms is a job that everyone has to do. For the typist, the task involves two activities.

1   SELECTING THE RIGHT INFORMATION

When people draft the data to be typed on a form, they often simply jot down notes, but not always in the same order as the form calls for them. For instance, at the top of their list they may write, 'Date the form for tomorrow', leaving the typist to look for the place for the date, which may be at the bottom of the form.

Read through the form before you insert it into the typewriter, checking the details that you have for entering against each heading. Make a note on the draft (a cross will do) against each item that has a separate heading on the form. The reason for doing this is to avoid typing details such as the post code with the address details, only to find when you move down the form there is a pre-printed heading 'post code'.

2   USING YOUR MACHINE

Typed wording has to be positioned on forms:

(a) alongside headings (e.g. references in letters and memos);
(b) over dotted lines;
(c) in boxes (e.g. figures in cheques);
(d) in columns (e.g. invoices).

You also have to be able to delete printed words (e.g. Mr/Miss/Mrs/Ms).

The variable line-spacer (usually a knob at the end of the cylinder) alters the positioning of typewriter lines. This will leave the single- or double-line spacing operating as normal, but with changed position on the paper.

The interliner (a lever usually near to the paper release) will free the line-spacing mechanism so that you can move the paper to any point within the normal line spacing. As soon as you return the interliner to the 'off' position, the line spacing returns to its original positioning.

Whichever method you use, the important thing to remember to do is to *check* before typing each line to make sure your entry will be in the right position.

When you have to delete words, make sure you do so effectively. The hyphen key does not cross out very well, nor does the underscore key, even if you raise it. A small or capital 'x' is the most effective.

IN THE EXAM

There will be one form to be completed. This may contain a variety of pre-printing, for example, dotted lines and boxes.

The information for completing the form will be given in handwriting on a different page or written directly on to a copy of the form.

You will not be asked to invent any information, or to supply extra data from your own knowledge. Therefore, if no information is given for any of the heading(s) on the form, you should leave the entry space blank.

The purpose of extending the checking procedure that you used in Part One (see page 11) is important. At this stage of your exam preparation you need to know if you are missing mistakes even though you are reading your work. If you are now getting someone else to sign your progress reports, this puts a *double responsibility on you* to make sure that there are no faults in your work. In the exam you will be on your own, and if **you** do not find faults, no one else can prevent your uncorrected work reaching the examiner and being penalised. So it is important to find out if you are going wrong, to make sure you improve, and to accept criticism in this light so that people are not unwilling to point out your faults for fear of you taking offence.

Some of the practice material will be more difficult than the tasks that will appear in the exam. It is always a good plan to be more than adequately prepared for any test so that if you are, at the beginning at least, a little nervous or in a strange environment, which for a while disturbs your concentration, you have the confidence of being well prepared.

Rule up your new progress report as follows:

Practice Material: Section No	Date first completed	Errors noted, and items needing attention	Work accurate and well displayed
1			Signed: Date:
2			Signed: Date:
3			Signed: Date:

It is worth thinking about using a variety of correcting materials, rather than just one. The eraser is better for correcting some errors. For example, a soft pencil rubber blots excess carbon from the copy so that you can make a clean correction more easily, while a pencil-shaped hard eraser is good for single letters within a word. Thin fluid is also good for single letters or whole words – but it is poor for carbon copies. Correcting paper is good if your ribbon is not too dark, but it is not the most effective way of correcting carbon copies, and the chalk can get rubbed off later if your work is likely to have other papers packed on top of it.

IN THE EXAM

There is no special test for this, but you will be expected to correct any errors that you may make.

There is no restriction on the various types of correcting materials that you may take with you to use. If you prefer, you may use a variety of methods.

Remember

It is important to correct the carbon copy. You will not be penalised if this is done by reinserting it into the machine and typing directly on to the copy. But you must get the carbon copy accurate, because faults left there will be counted as word faults if they have been corrected only on the top copy.

WHAT THE EXAMINER WILL LOOK FOR

√ no dirty marks
√ corrections not immediately noticeable
√ all errors found and corrected cleanly
BUT
! characters appearing blurred or bold in contrast with uncorrected work – when, for instance, you have typed on fluid before it is properly dry
! smoothness of paper impaired, e.g. creases made by a rubber or lumpy correcting fluid used
! substantial misalignment of characters, i.e. correction typed half a line space or more above or below the original line
! hole in the paper unless already penalised as a word fault, e.g. a hole caused by erasing a word/character from the margin

Note:
Words that have omitted characters or spaces within them (including omissions caused by faulty use of correction materials/techniques, e.g. hole in paper or character(s) left illegible by correcting material) will be penalised as word faults (see B1.2 on page 7).

Stationery is a large expense in most businesses, and typists who frequently scrap envelopes, printed letterheads and forms are not popular.

It is not, of course, good practice to send out work that is shoddy or on the wrong stationery simply in order to save paper. Nevertheless, you should practise with the aim of re-typing any task only rarely, and never more than once.

Your employer will expect you to know which stationery is appropriate for the task you have been asked to do. It is very unlikely that handwritten work will be marked with instructions when to use letterheads and memo forms, although it will be necessary for you to be told if a particular size of paper must be used, even though the work looks as if it would normally fit a smaller size.

You will also be expected to use stationery sensibly. For instance, letterheads and memo forms often have headings such as 'Date' or 'Our ref', and you should practise getting the right data in the right place, as well as generally using the stationery to make your work look attractive.

It is a good idea to notice, after you have typed each task during practice, how long the draft looked and how well it fitted on to the paper with the margins you used. Gradually, you will develop your own judgement so that you will be able to estimate what margins and line spacing to use in order to balance the space around your work.

IN THE EXAM

The answer book provided for you in the exam will contain the following:
1   *Two sheets of A4 letterhead.*   There will be one A4 letter in each exam. No A5 letter will be included.
2   *Two sheets of A4 memo paper.*   There will be one memo in each exam. Even though this may be short enough to fit on A5 paper, since you have none available you must type the memo on the A4 paper provided. There is no need to fold or tear this to make it A5. If you do tear or fold the paper unsuccessfully, leaving jagged tearing or careless unsightly creasing, you risk being penalised.
3   *Four sheets of A4 plain white paper.*
4   *Two sheets of A5 plain white paper.*   The A5 size will be supplied in the form of one A4 sheet perforated across the centre. If you separate them, take care not to tear other than along the perforation.
5   *Two sheets of A4 yellow flimsy paper*   for taking carbon copy (plus one spare sheet in case you need to make a second attempt).
6   *One DL manilla envelope.*   One envelope will be required in each exam. You will need to take special care as this is the one task for which there is no 'reserve' stationery.
7   *In the exam paper, two copies of a printed form*   for completion, without carbon copy, with details given on a separate page in the exam paper. The form is perforated for you to remove it for typing; and is printed on both sides in case you need to re-type. Again, take care not to tear the paper other than along the perforation.

With the exception of the envelope, there is enough stationery for you to re-type each task in case you should find it necessary.

You will need to provide your own carbon paper to make one copy of one task.

You should practise making corrections to your work until you can do so well enough for your amendments to be unnoticeable at first glance.

Whether you use an eraser, paper/plastic sheets or fluid, you will need *patience*. No method can be effective if rushed.

Remember to be gentle! Scrubbing the paper with an eraser will produce a hole – or, at the very least, remove the surface of the paper to leave an obvious mark.

Over-use or too heavy pressure on paper or plastic film sheet can damage the characters on either side of the correction.

Too heavy application of fluid will be noticeable, particularly if the fluid is lumpy or too thick.

When you are using a machine with lift-off tape, keep the pressure switch to minimum unless you have a good reason for extra pressure, for example, you are producing carbon copies or typing masters for duplicating.

So when using any of these materials and techniques, work slowly and use only enough pressure to remove the wrong character(s) – too much will destroy your efforts. *Watch out for dirty marks* – check your fingers are clean and dry before holding work steady against the cylinder for correcting.

CORRECTING CARBON COPIES

If you have the patience and the time to correct the carbon copy *at the same time* as correcting the original, so much the better. You will then not forget to do it.

Protect your carbon copy while you correct the top copy.

When using the small sheets of plastic correcting film or the paper varieties, you can obtain a special type for use with carbon copies, so that you can correct the error on top and the copy at the same time.

If you use fluid, you can also correct the carbon and top copies at the same time – but you will need *patience* to allow the fluid to dry properly, particularly on the carbon copy. Otherwise, two things will happen: firstly, the correction on the carbon copy will be unreadable; secondly, wet fluid transfers to the carbon paper, dries, and when you use it again your next carbon copy will have blanks because there is no carbon left to make an impression on some of the lines.

When using an eraser, you should be careful not to allow the rubbing on the top copy to make its impression through the carbon paper; so insert a piece of paper between the coated side of the carbon paper and your copy until you have completed erasing the mistake on the original. Then you can rub out the error on the carbon copy. Apart from the need to go slowly and gently to avoid smudging, you must also remember to *remove the protecting paper* before typing in the correction.

If you have a machine fitted with lift-off tape, you will find it time-consuming to correct a carbon copy at the same time as correcting the original. Nevertheless, you will find it worth while, if you have to correct two or three words, to slip a protecting paper between the carbon paper and your copy while you make the correction with the lift-off tape. This will avoid overtyping on the carbon copy, which is more difficult to remove later. But do remember to take away the protecting paper before typing the rest of your task. After the document is removed from the machine you can then correct the carbon copy using fluid (or an eraser), reinserting it into the typewriter and typing in the correct words.

Check instructions carefully for any special requirements for a particular size of paper to be used. Set aside paper for this task to make sure you do not use it all on other tasks.

Note:
No extra stationery will be allowed for use during the exam.

WHAT THE EXAMINER WILL LOOK FOR
Presentation

√ correct stationery used. *Note:* If you should spoil the envelope or second sheets of printed stationery, re-type the task on plain white paper. This will count as one presentation fault – whereas if you fail to complete the task, you will not be able to pass, since you will not have completed the work set and worked at the required rate of production (see Part Three).

4   COMPLIMENTARY CLOSE AND SIGNATORY

It is impossible to make a firm rule about exactly how much space is needed for the signature of the person sending a letter.

If you do not know how large a signature may be, a good rule to practise is to leave four clear lines, that is, turn up five single line spaces after the complimentary close (e.g. Yours faithfully) before typing the name of the person signing the letter. For example:

```
Yours faithfully
PRAXITELES GROUP

(4 clear lines)



J G Denworthy
Financial Controller
```

or

```
Yours sincerely


(4 clear lines)


L C Blenkins
```

In letters that are to be sent to a number of people, the sender's name is sometimes typed instead of signed. For example:

```
Yours faithfully
PRAXITELES GROUP

J G Denworthy

Financial Controller
```

Each organisation has its own house style for letters, including complimentary closings, and you will need to find out what these are when starting work in an office.

IN THE EXAM

You will always be told which complimentary close to use, but as these are included in the words you are expected to spell (see B4 on page 4), they will often be abbreviated.

The name of the company (e.g. Praxiteles Group) will not always be included, and you should *not* add a name if one is not shown in the draft. You should also *copy* details included in the draft of the sender's name and job title – do not add any words not shown.

Remember

If the note 'Enc' is to be included it must be placed below the signature. Leave space for the signature and then turn up two more line spaces before typing 'Enc', *or* if the name of the sender and/or job title are included, leave at least one clear line space after them before typing 'Enc'.

WHAT THE EXAMINER WILL LOOK FOR

Presentation

! *no* space left for the signature
! *no* space above and below a typed signatory's name in a circular

As well as being able to use the typewriter, you will need to be able to handle paper, including carbon paper, without allowing your finished work to become dirty or crumpled. *All it takes is care.*

If you type for yourself you can measure the importance of good presentation. When you are employed as a typist, you will be typing for other people, who will be insulted if you think their work is of so little importance that it does not matter if it looks shoddy. Poorly finished work, if it is sent out, may give a bad impression of your firm. On the other hand, your employer will probably complain if you are always wasting stationery through re-typing. So you need to keep clean and keep your work clean.

CLEAN HABITS

1   *Carbon paper.*   Use plastic varieties if possible to reduce likelihood of smudging. If only the 'soft' carbon paper is available, always keep the carbon-coated side facing away from you. Use the paper release when inserting it into the machine so as to avoid unnecessary smudging of the copy paper. Always touch and hold carbon paper *gently* – pressing or gripping it will make it smudge.

2   *Thumbprints.*   If your hands get warm, they will pick up dust very easily and leave stains on papers. Keep tissues handy and use them often. Hold papers *gently*. Do not press down too hard when holding paper steady to make corrections.

3   Have your own places for:
(a) *unused stationery*. Cover it up to protect it;
(b) *completed work*. Get it well out of harm's way, perfectly flat, with protecting paper underneath as well as on top. Always wipe your fingers on tissue before picking it up when you need to handle it;
(c) *carbon paper*. Don't trust it! Keep it well away from your typewriter, completed work, and unused stationery;
(d) *correcting materials.* If you use an eraser, make sure that it is not resting on a desk so that when you want it you have to feel for it under paper, shuffle papers to get at it – or even have to pick it up from the floor and risk more dirt! Have a place up off the desk or floor – on a string round your neck, if you like, or in your pocket, or in a drawer, but lying on the desk is a dangerous place for an eraser!

If you use correcting plastic film or paper sheets the same applies – don't risk losing them under papers on the desk. Have a special place for them – under the typewriter, in a drawer, inside your dictionary, anywhere that is handy and clean, but keep them away from your work.

Always replace stoppers on correcting fluid! Have a special place again – so much time is wasted in searching for the bottle, and in looking for it you can knock it over and damage stationery or completed work.

CREASING

It can happen:
1   when inserting paper into the typewriter – so don't rush it. Make sure the bail (the bar with rubber rollers which holds the paper

EXTRACT - ADVERTISEMENT DRAFT

We are currently operating a Work Experience programme for
students ~~with~~ /in the/ advanced stages of their secretarial training.
~~The~~ /Our W — E — differs from others/ programme ~~is based on similar ones~~ in that it does not
rely on ~~em~~ students going into the ~~employers~~ offices /of local employers/ for
one or two weeks to take part in the ~~employers a~~ integral
adtivities of their business.

Instead, our students operate the PRAXITELES GROUP OFFICE
SERVICES* - a mini company which under/takes ~~contract work~~
on a contract basis for /Small businesses/ ~~xm employees~~ in the area. This work
includes text processing: letters from handwritten drafts
                                  including circulars/mail shots
                          : ~~dictatioed material~~ /audio-typing - for which our equipment can be hired/

                          : ~~draft~~ reports from draft to ~~completi~~
                              completion stage

            book-keeping : including VAT records
            photocopying

If you are operating a small business, and are ~~wondering~~ /considering/ how
best to cope with ~~the office~~ your growing needs for book-keeping
and typing, eg invoicing, ~~then~~ please give us an opportunity to
assist you thro' this service. Give us a ring on 0425-1022847.
~~We will arrange with you an appointment~~ to tell us when you'd
like to come in to our office in Hansomth Way or when you'd like
us to come to your office to talk to you.

---

* A company limited by guarantee

against the roller) is out of the way. When using envelopes, or sets of papers and carbon, use the paper release and gently 'push' materials into position before taking off the paper release.

2   through crumpling paper when picking it up – go *gently*!

3   if you fold paper carelessly – so don't fold unnecessarily.

TEARING

Handle perforated sheets carefully. Always separate *gently* and accurately.

Machines with moving carriages can tear paper when returning from extreme left or right after, say, correcting if the paper is allowed to flap forward. Always be sure your cardholder and paper bail are in position to hold your work firmly against the cylinder.

Do not deliberately tear stationery, for example, to make A4 into A5.

IN THE EXAM

Accidents will happen! You can see from the chapter on stationery (page 53) that there is enough stationery in the exam folder to allow for one re-typing should any of your work get spoilt (excepting the envelope).

There is no need to fold A4 stationery for work which does not fill the page, so avoid the risk of dirtying your work.

You should never tear stationery – so do not risk penalty through mistakes made by doing this. The stationery that is supplied in A4 sheets perforated across the centre (plain white A5) should be carefully separated at the perforation.

Keep tissues handy to wipe your fingers before separating and handling stationery – and work gently because pressure may leave fingermarks.

Take special care with carbons – particularly when correcting (see pages 104 – 5).

Use clean stationery. Typing on both sides of the paper is not encouraged, but if you have spoilt the rest of your paper, it is better to type on the back of another task rather than fail the exam for not completing all of the work (see also 'What the examiner will look for' on page 54).

WHAT THE EXAMINER WILL LOOK FOR
Presentation

√ clean work – no dirty marks

√ no creases – there is no need to fold A4 paper, but there will not be a penalty for a careful, neat fold

√ no tearing – separation of perforated sheets neatly will not, of course, be called 'tearing'

Task 53

The Investment Club has determined that the revenue from 1986 contributions shall be invested in 7-day ordinary shares. // The rate of interest on this type of share ranges between 7.3% and 10.1%* depending on the building society chosen. The Secy is currently making a survey in anticipation of members' agreement in principle to this procedure. // The intention is that further contributions from 1987 wl. be added to the a/c. until the total reaches the minimum required for investment in a 90-day a/c., which is at present £2000.*

* These figures as at time of writing; not g'teed.

Task 54

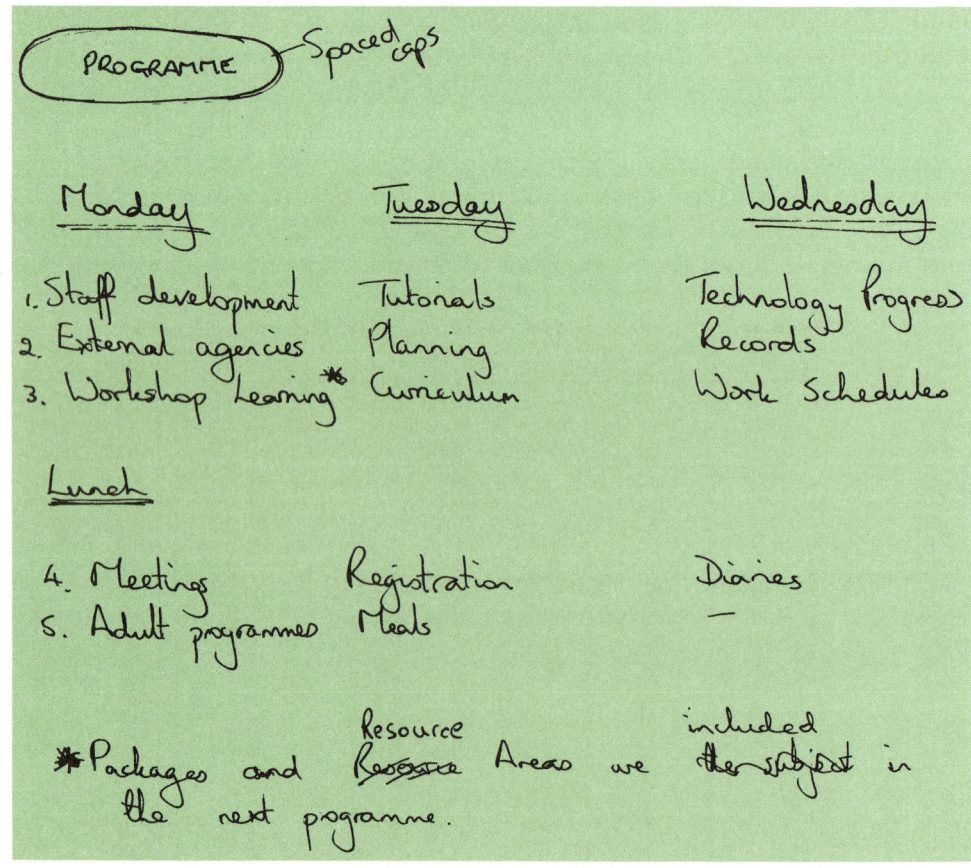

PROGRAMME — Spaced caps

Monday	Tuesday	Wednesday
1. Staff development	Tutorials	Technology Progress
2. External agencies	Planning	Records
3. Workshop Learning*	Curriculum	Work Schedules

Lunch

| 4. Meetings | Registration | Diaries |
| 5. Adult programmes | Meals | — |

*Packages and Resource Areas we included the subject in the next programme.

Consistency

(a) ABBREVIATIONS FOR MEASUREMENTS
WEIGHTS/TIMES/MONEY

> Measurements can now be expressed as: 25 mm (1") and 1 m (approx. 3' 3").
>
> Vegetables were packed in sacks weighing 1 cwt but tinned goods were labelled "150 g and 200 g".
>
> We ordered taxis for 1000 hrs at the hotel and 1430 hrs at the airport.
>
> The rate of exchange varied between BF 74 and BF 76 to £1.

In business it is essential to type numbers accurately. Style of presentation is of secondary importance, but it is good practice to use the same style throughout a document – and this is the sort of refinement that distinguishes an excellent typist from the average.

When working from handwritten drafts, it is often difficult to tell whether the writer has used spaces around abbreviations. For example:

> The carpet will be 16 m x 4.3 m and we are ordering curtains today for the windows 3 m x 2 m & 1.5 m x 90 cm.

Or one particular style may be required in an organisation (the 'house style'). For example:

> The carpet will be 16m x 4.3m and we are ordering
> curtains today for the windows 3m x 2m and 1.5m x 90cm.

Or you may be used to leaving a space between the figure and the measure. For example:

> The carpet will be 16 m x 4.3 m and we are ordering
> curtains today for the windows 3 m x 2 m and 1.5 m x 90 cm.

3 FOOTNOTES

You should leave at least one clear line space to separate a footnote from the main body of the document. The reason for this is that a footnote is simply an added piece of information that does not need to be included in the main text. Without a clear line space it could look as though it were part of the text above, and so confuse the reader.

In the Report* there
are several references
to major repairs wh.
wl. be undertaken next
yr.

* Issued by HMSO, Aug
1985

In the Report* there are
several references to major
repairs which will be undertaken next year.

* Issued by HMSO, Aug 1985

IN THE EXAM

Only one footnote will be included. This may be marked in the text by a figure one typed one half-line space above your typing line or by an asterisk (*), which is included on the keyboard of most typewriters. If you do not have a key to print this 'star' you should combine the small 'x' and '–' keys, typed one half space above your typing line.

Remember

You should not leave a space after the word in the text where the footnote is marked. When you type the footnote at the bottom of the text you will not be penalised if no space appears after the asterisk or raised figure one. You may leave a space if you wish. You will be penalised if the figure one is not raised one half-line space above your typing line.

WHAT THE EXAMINER WILL LOOK FOR

Accuracy

! Omission of the symbol in the text or with the footnote
! Omission of any separating line shown in the draft

Note:
There is no need for you to insert a line *not* shown in the draft.

Presentation

√ at least one clear line space before the footnote is typed
√ at least one clear line space before and after any separating line

The important point is that you should be consistent, that is, stick to the same way throughout the document. An example of *lack of care* and *inconsistency* is:

> The carpet will be 16m x 4.3 m and we are ordering
> curtains today for the windows 3 mx 2 m and 1.5 m x 90cm.

(b) WORDS OR FIGURES

There are no hard and fast rules about whether to type numbers in words or figures, but it can be distracting to a reader if:

(i) sentences start with figures, for example, '1 of us will be at the party'; or

(ii) complex numbers are written in words, for example, 'We stock two hundred and seventy-eight lines of gardening goods'.

   If the work from which you are copying contains a mixture of figures and numbers, you will want to decide which style to use. To help you, check to see if

(i) any sentences begin with a number;

(ii) numbers in the text are long-winded in words.

If any sentences begin with a number, type *all* numbers in words.

> *There will be 4 of our employees attending the conference. One of them will be the Managing Director.*
>
> There will be four of our employees attending the conference. One of them will be the Managing Director.

If numbers in the text are long-winded in words, type all numbers in figures.

> *The eight invoices covered 4 separate deliveries of these items comprising 678 cases of toys.*
>
> The 8 invoices covered 4 separate deliveries of these items comprising 678 cases of toys.

If any sentences begin with a number, but the draft also contains long numbers, you should judge for yourself whether the wording could be slightly altered to avoid starting a sentence with a figure. You will not have to make such a decision in the Stage I exam, since you will be able to copy work as it is presented in the draft.

(c) WORDS OR SYMBOLS

It is unlikely that you will need to change what has been written for you

C10 *Practice material*

Task 51

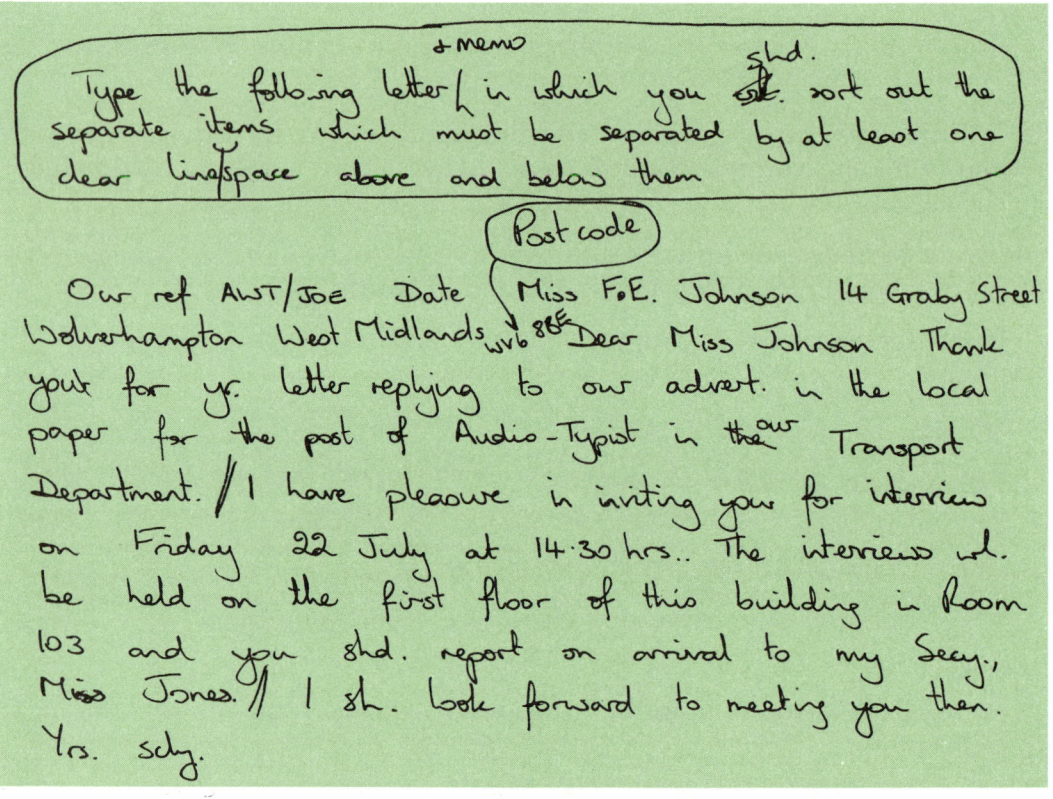

+ Memo

Type the following letter, in which you shd. sort out the separate items which must be separated by at least one clear line/space above and below them

Post code

Our ref AWT/JOE   Date   Miss F.E. Johnson   14 Graby Street Wolverhampton West Midlands, WV6 8EE Dear Miss Johnson Thank you for yr. letter replying to our advert. in the local paper for the post of Audio-Typist in the our Transport Department. // I have pleasure in inviting you for interview on Friday 22 July at 14.30 hrs.. The interview wl. be held on the first floor of this building in Room 103 and you shd. report on arrival to my Secy., Miss Jones. // I sh. look forward to meeting you then. Yrs. scly.

Task 52

Memo to Chief Accountant   From Publicity Officer
South Park Project
I wd. like yr. opinion on the attached copy of our proposed Press Release. I intend to put this before the Board at our next meeting. // I am still waiting for the estimate from Turner Brothers about the additional seating. I contacted them by telephone this morning + they have promised me the figures for Mon. // The draft report on costs is excellent.

to copy, but the writer may mix up words and symbols, and then you will need to use one or the other and stick to it:

Per cent or %

Although 50 per cent of the students passed this examination only 10 per cent gained distinction.

This may be presented as:

Although 50 per cent of the students passed this examination only 10 per cent gained distinction.	*or*	Although 50% of the students passed this examination only 10% gained distinction.

Pounds or £

We asked for a rebate of £10 but the Authority allowed only £2.

This may be presented as:

We asked for a rebate of £10 but the Authority allowed only £2.	*or*	We asked for a rebate of ten pounds but the Authority allowed only two pounds.

Dollars or $

We paid approximately $5 for an article originally valued around $20.

This may be presented as:

We paid approximately $5 for an article originally valued around $20.	*or*	We paid approximately 5 dollars for an article originally valued around 20 dollars.

Feet and inches symbols

The pelmets were 7'6" long to fit window frames which were 7'1".

1   PARAGRAPHS

It is *essential* to leave at least one clear line space between paragraphs. When typing paragraphs in single-line spacing this clear line will show the separation of paragraphs very clearly.

When typing in double-line spacing, it is customary to leave an extra clear line to mark new paragraphs. However, some offices do not require this, and if you do not usually leave an extra space between paragraphs when typing in double-line spacing, you will not be penalised for following your usual practice in the exam.

IN THE EXAM

There will be no special test of this point, but you will be expected to *leave a clear line space between paragraphs.*

You will be penalised if you sometimes leave one clear line space and sometimes leave more within the same document (see C3 Consistency on page 70).

WHAT THE EXAMINER WILL LOOK FOR

Presentation

√   at least one clear line space between paragraphs

2   HEADINGS AND DOCUMENTS

You should learn to leave at least one clear line space to separate the different parts of any document. In letters, the different parts that need separating are: references, date, address, opening (salutation), paragraphs, closing (complimentary close) and enclosure mark. Headings also need to be separately presented, and it may be that you would wish to add the refinement of extra space after main headings.

IN THE EXAM

You may copy the spacing implied by the drafts. You will not be penalised if you do, or do not leave *extra* line space(s) before and after separate items, but you must leave at least *one* line clear when no instructions are given.

Remember

Watch out for any instructions to leave clear a given number of line spaces. If you do not follow such instructions you will be penalised for one presentation fault.

This may be presented as:

<table>
<tr><td>The pelmets were 7'6" long to fit window frames which were 7'1".</td><td>or</td><td>The pelmets were 7 ft 6 in long to fit window frames which were 7 ft 1 in.</td></tr>
</table>

Note:
All these symbols are used only with figures. If the text uses words instead of figures then any accompanying symbol should be replaced by a word, for example, 'Ten pounds' *or* '£10' but *not* 'ten £'.

IN THE EXAM

It is perfectly all right for you to copy the work just as it appears in the exam paper. There is no deliberate test of whether you will use a particular style. The syllabus allows you to decide matters such as spacing. This is in case you can't be sure what spacing has been used in the handwritten task, or because you may be in a job where you type these items in a house style using different spacing from the writer of the exam. The syllabus does, however, instruct you to stick to one style throughout a document.

The exam tasks will not include inconsistencies for you to put right. You may follow what you see, but you can choose your own style if preferred as long as it is used consistently.

Remember

It is particularly important that numbers should be 100 per cent accurate. In business any error in figures could be costly. Style is of secondary importance to accuracy.

WHAT THE EXAMINER WILL LOOK FOR

Accuracy

! inaccurate figures or numbers (each number or group of figures will count as a word fault)

Presentation

√ same spacing and method used to present each type of data

Note:
One presentation fault will be counted for inconsistency in each type of data. For example, if measurements are presented inconsistently within a task, one fault: if numbers are presented inconsistently within the same task, a second fault.

Margins

For typed work to be usable, it must be sensibly presented and placed on the paper, as well as being accurate.

With experience, you will develop skill in selecting margins (as well as line spacing) to present work attractively on different sizes of paper.

However, as a beginner it is best not to spend a long time counting and calculating for this purpose. You need to develop and follow general rules until you are able to judge the length and type of work that does not fit your rules and results in, say, a great expanse of unused paper with work looking as if it is sitting on a shelf at the top.

A general rule you could follow is:

25 mm (1 in.) margins all round for plain A4
13 mm (½ in.) margins all round for plain A5

'All round' means top and both sides, but when you are typing *long* documents likely to extend more than one page, 'all round' includes the bottom margin. Make a pencil mark in your margin approximately 50 mm (2 in.) from the bottom of the page as advance warning and a reminder not to type beyond 25 mm (1 in.) from the bottom edge.

When you are able to judge that the length of the text may be rather *short* for this rule, you can extend your margins to 38 mm (1½ in.) for A4 and 25 mm (1 in.) for A5 paper for this 'special' task.

A general rule for use of printed stationery is to align your left margin with that used by the printer and to leave at least one clear line space after the lowest printed item. Right-hand margins are safest set at 13 mm (½ in.) so that the 'bell' allows you space to complete typing any word you have started before returning for the next line.

IN THE EXAM

Remember

1   Check for instructions to leave specified margins. (Each exam will contain an instruction to leave specified space *either* as a margin *or* within typing lines.)
2   Take care when assembling and loading sets of paper for carbon copying (that is, top sheet, carbon and flimsy paper). Your margin on the carbon copy could be less than on your top sheet if the sheets are not aligned.

WHAT THE EXAMINER WILL LOOK FOR

Presentation

√   In the absence of instructions, margins will not be penalised unless there is less than 13 mm (½ in.) at top or left.

Tasks 23 – 26 are typical of the kind of documents containing abbreviations for measurements/weights/times/money that you would be given in an office. Type these, remembering to pay careful attention to presentation *and* accuracy.

Task 23

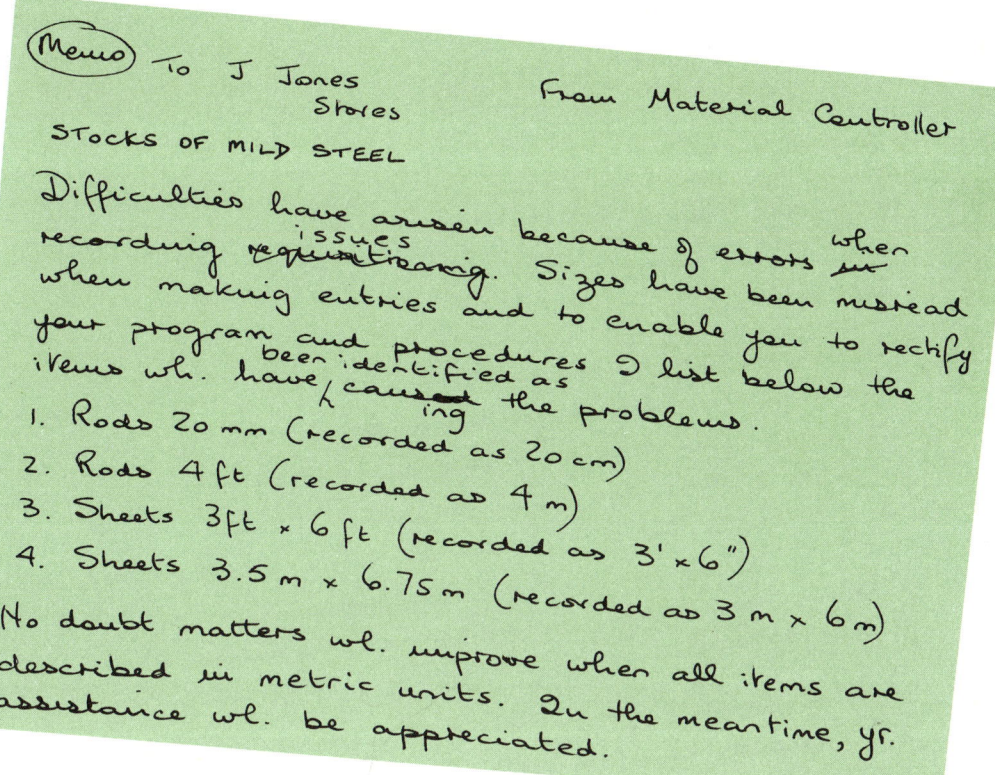

(Memo) To J Jones
                Stores   From Material Controller

STOCKS OF MILD STEEL

Difficulties have arisen because of errors when recording issues ~~requisitioning~~. Sizes have been misread when making entries and to enable you to rectify your program and procedures I list below the items wh. have been identified as causing the problems.

1. Rods 20 mm (recorded as 20 cm)
2. Rods 4 ft (recorded as 4 m)
3. Sheets 3ft x 6 ft (recorded as 3' x 6")
4. Sheets 3.5 m x 6.75 m (recorded as 3 m x 6 m)

No doubt matters wl. improve when all items are described in metric units. In the meantime, yr. assistance wl. be appreciated.

Task 24

Aide Memoire for 4 pm Tuesday

The laden weight of all our vehicles is within 30 tonnes. We have registration certificates issued by the gov. wh. confirm this and are available for inspection at any time. Please confirm whether we shd. bring such documents at the time of our appt. to discuss final details ~~at a meeting~~ next week. // The suggestion that 50 tonnes is our limit is ~~are~~ not acceptable. We have held ~~never~~ licences for approx. 10 yrs. + have never owned vehicles of that weight.

(Letter - to be dated this month + year only (no day))

Our ref: CARSUR

(Leave 9 clear lines for address to be inserted later)

Dr. Sir/Madam

I am writing to ask yr. help in a study wh. we have been asked to undertake on behalf of Praxi. Yr. name has been (randomly) selected as part of a small sample of those who have bought a Praxi car in the past 4 yrs. // Both the co. & its dealers are vitally interested in providing you w. the best possible standard of servicing & they are concerned to know what you have to say about the servicing of yr. car.

I think you will find the enclosed questionnaire interesting, easy to follow & simple to complete. In most cases all you are requested to do is to tick an appropriate box.

The information will be used by

Inset & spaces

1. Praxi Car Sales
2. Praxi Servicing
3. Praxi Travel Agencies
4. Praxi Finance Services

Yours sely.

(Thanking you in advance for yr. help.)

From Education + Training   To
                    Section   Sales Manager

There are 7 different programmes wh. can be offered
for short courses to bring our representatives up to
date on the new products to be launched last next month.
These are listed in the attached brochure, and
We wd. call yr. attention to the 3 different timings
wh. can also be offered for each of the programmes,
as follows:-

Monday - Wednesday   10 am - 4 pm

Tuesday - Thurs.   11 am - 5pm

Wed. - Fri.   5.30   9pm
                            6 pm - 8pm

Messrs W Pickering Ltd

Derby House

Twelling Lane

BARNSLEY Yorks BY71 4TW

Dr. Sirs

Thank you for yr. ye inquiry of last week. We are pleased
to inform you that, contrary to our telephone call
last yesterday, we can now quote for 3 of the 8 items
you require:

1 doz boxes Clips 12 mm x 2 mm   £15.00

8 cartons Bolts 12 cm x 5 mm   72.75

5 packets Washers (small)   2.33

Yrs. ffly.

IN THE EXAM

One task in each exam will include an instruction to leave space *either* as a margin *or* within the typing lines.

You will always be told the size of the space to be allocated. This size may be given as a measurement (e.g. 50 mm) or as a number of line spaces (e.g. 12 lines).

Instructions using measurements will ask for *at least* the given measurement to be left clear – so if you are not absolutely sure how many letters or lines make up the measurement required, try to leave a little *extra* space rather than risk your space being too short.

Remember

When instructions say a definite number of lines must be left clear, then count carefully the number of 'returns' you make and be sure to turn up an extra one after the number given in the instruction. This means that if you are asked to 'leave 12 lines clear' you must not type on the twelfth line, but on the thirteenth.

WHAT THE EXAMINER WILL LOOK FOR

Accuracy

! any word inaccurate, including following punctuation and spacing

Presentation

√ space across the page equal to or more than the measurement given
√ space down the page equal to or more than the measurement given
√ *or* the *exact* number of line spaces requested to be left clear

C8 *Practice material*

Task 49

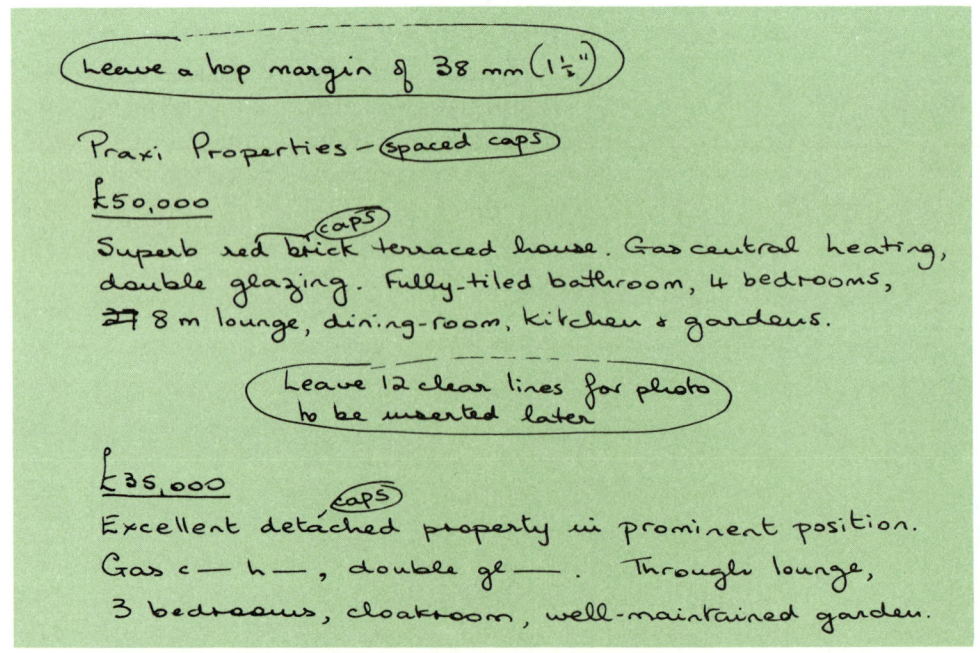

(d) PUNCTUATION

You will be used to seeing letters and memos typed with either open or full punctuation. The following examples highlight the differences between them.

OPEN PUNCTUATION:	FULL PUNCTUATION:
24 January 1986	24th January, 1986
Mr J A Turne 56 High Street Drews Laneton Leicester LS2 41A	Mr. J. A. Turne, 56, High Street, Drews Laneton, Leicester, LS2 41A.
Dear Mr Turne	Dear Mr. Turne,
As requested, we now enclose your diary left with us last week.	As requested, we now enc-lose your diary left with us last week.
We shall hope, before long, to see you and your wife again.	We shall hope, before long, to see you and your wife again.
Yours sincerely JAMES & BULL	Yours sincerely, JAMES & BULL,
A G Andrews Sales Assistant	A. G. Andrews, Sales Assistant.
Enc	Enc.

It is important to be consistent in the use of punctuation and spacing after it. For example, if you insert a comma at the end of the first line of an address, you should include a comma at the end of each following line, with a full stop at the end (full punctuation). Should any other address(es) be included in the same document, they should also have the same style of punctuation. If you choose to use no commas in the address (open punctuation), then you should not use a full stop at the end or insert punctuation in any other address(es) included in the same document.

Note:
Punctuation within the body of a letter is not normally affected since it is grammatically necessary; but when dates occur you should use the same style as you use at the top of the document for the date (see B1 on page 12).

When you are using punctuation, at least one space should be left clear after each mark. It is common practice to leave two or three clear spaces after a full stop marking the end of a sentence (to indicate a longer pause for the reader).

Open punctuation is a much quicker style to use and has few rules to be remembered. One is that if you have separate items on the same line (e.g. town and postcode), you need to leave at least two spaces between

KNOW YOUR MACHINE

One of the techniques of a competent typist is to use the typewriter as a measuring instrument.

Down the page

Six typewriting lines equal 25 mm (1 in.). There are very few exceptions to this. Most typewriters will turn up $\frac{1}{6}$ in. (4.23 mm) at each 'return'.
    Once you know this it is easy to act on instructions such as:

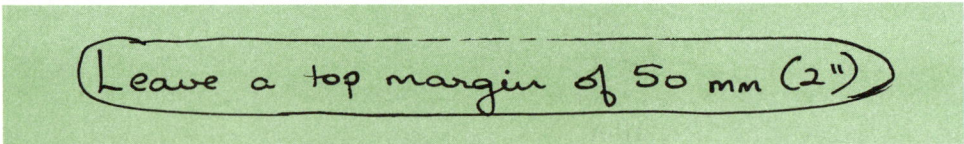

Leave a top margin of 50 mm (2")

by using the 'return' lever or key and counting the line spaces so that you leave twelve clear and type on the thirteenth.

Across the page ('pitch')

It is not so easy to provide a general measurement for the number of letters making up 25 mm (1 in.) across the page. The best way to be sure is to measure it, using a ruler. In most cases, there will be twelve characters (or spaces) to 25 mm (1 in.), that is, 12-pitch, but some will be 10-pitch, and others 11-pitch. So when you change machines, it is worth checking.

BUSINESS PRACTICE

When you receive instructions in an office about your typewriting work, they may include requests such as:

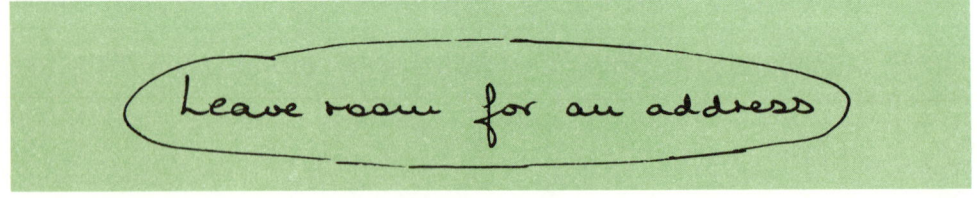

Leave room for an address

This, of course, means you have to decide, using your knowledge of business practice, how much space to allocate.
    Such an instruction will suggest that the document you are to type will be sent to more than one address. This means that you will need to leave space for the longest (rather than the shortest) general address normally used, that is, five lines plus at least one clear line above and one line below the address, seven clear lines in all.

them (in place of a comma) to avoid their being read together as if part of a sentence. It is not good practice to leave too many spaces (for instance, more than six) because the words would then not be connected by the reader even as a list.

IN THE EXAM

If you normally use full punctuation in your work, it is not necessary to change to open punctuation – and vice versa. The syllabus allows you to use which style is more familiar to you.

This means that there is no special test of consistency in use of punctuation, and the paper will not be designed to include particular styles to test your knowledge of them.

Instead, the syllabus instructs you to be consistent as to *when* you use punctuation (other than when it is grammatically necessary) and *how many* spaces you use after punctuation. For instance, if you choose to leave two or three spaces after full stops at ends of sentences, you should leave the same number after each full stop in the task.

WHAT THE EXAMINER WILL LOOK FOR

Accuracy

! no space at all after punctuation marks

Presentation

√ same number of spaces after punctuation marks (a) within sentences, and (b) after full stops
√ open *or* full punctuation used consistently within the task

Mrs E Watson 25 Woodland Road
DERBY DE2 8NE

Ref Js/To

Dr. Mr Watson

SMITH v. WATSON

On my return from holiday I recd. yr. letter with regard to the above.

Mr Smith has stated that the following repairs have been undertaken **completed**:-

<u>January</u> 1980 - Repairs to the roof.

<u>February</u> 1981 - Replacement of roof to outside store and garage, as well as new paving of pathway into rear yard.

<u>August</u> 1983 - Rebuilding of outside yard wall at Market Street boundary.

<u>September</u> 1985 - Chimneys demolished and removed.

Will you please confirm that you agree the above work was carried out with your full knowledge and consent.

Yours ffly.

J Sutcliffe
Solicitor

(e) PARAGRAPHING

There are two types of paragraphs: blocked and indented. Whichever style you choose, you should use consistently.

Blocked   *Indented*

```
We shall be glad if you will        We shall be glad if
let us have details of your     you will let us have
accounts before we proceed      details of your accounts
to check these items.           before we proceed to check
                                these items.

Your early reply would be           Your early reply
appreciated so that the         would be appreciated so
matter can be finalised         that the matter can be
before the end of this month.   finalised before the end
                                of this month.
```

With headings

```
Autumn Sales                    Autumn Sales

These are increasingly popu-        These are increasing-
lar with our customers.         ly popular with our
                                customers.

Following the summer holidays,      Following the summer
they brighten up shopping       holidays, they brighten up
before the Xmas prepara-        shopping before the Xmas
tions.                          preparations.
```

Numbered

```
1.  We may not be able to       1       We may not be able
    supply you with blue                to supply you with blue
    bonnets at the same                 bonnets at the same
    price as yellow ones.               price as yellow ones.

2.  Delivery dates would not    2.          Delivery dates
    be affected.                        would not be affected.
```

and

```
  i) Winter items at 10% dis-   i)          Winter items at
     count.                             10% discount.

 ii) Goods from our autumn      ii)         Goods from our
     catalogue available                autumn catalogue
     immediately.                       available immediately.

iii) Summer clothes delivered   iii)        Summer clothes
     within six weeks.                  delivered within six
                                        weeks.
```

Note:
Roman numerals may be ranged to the right or left as shown in the two examples above – see also material in columns on page 74.

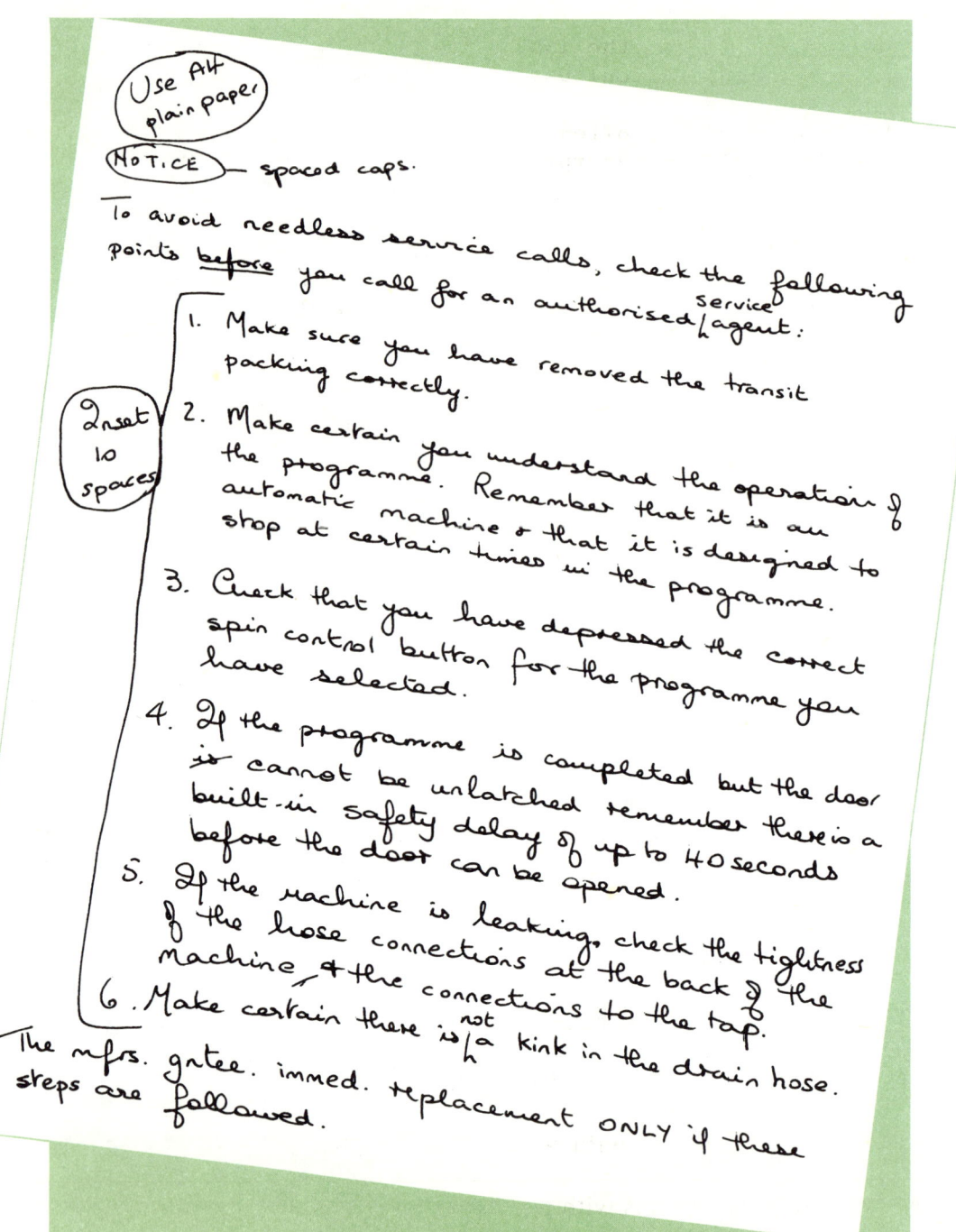

(Use A4 plain paper)

(NOTICE) — spaced caps.

To avoid needless service calls, check the following points before you call for an authorised service agent:

(Inset 10 spaces)

1. Make sure you have removed the transit packing correctly.

2. Make certain you understand the operation of the programme. Remember that it is an automatic machine & that it is designed to stop at certain times in the programme.

3. Check that you have depressed the correct spin control button for the programme you have selected.

4. If the programme is completed but the door is cannot be unlatched remember there is a built-in safety delay of up to 40 seconds before the door can be opened.

5. If the machine is leaking, check the tightness of the hose connections at the back of the machine, & the connections to the tap.

6. Make certain there is not a kink in the drain hose.

The mfrs. gntee. immed. replacement ONLY if these steps are followed.

```
a)   Try to follow the ins-      a)   Try to follow the
     tructions meticulously.          instructions meticulously.

b)   The matter is often         b)   The matter is often
     difficult to interpret.          difficult to interpret.


                                 a.        Try to follow the
                                           instructions meticu-
                                           lously.

                                 b.        The matter is
                                           often difficult to
                                           interpret.
```

When paragraphs are numbered or lettered, as above, leave at least one clear space before starting each paragraph.

IN THE EXAM

You may follow the style of paragraphing shown in the draft.
  Every effort is made to write clearly, but if you are unsure about the paragraphing used, *remember*:

- blocked paragraphs are always acceptable;
- each paragraph is a separate item (and so needs at least one clear line space before and after it).

This will help you to make sure that there is the minimum of one clear line space before and after each paragraph, and also that there is at least one clear space between numbering or lettering and the beginning of the paragraph.

WHAT THE EXAMINER WILL LOOK FOR

Presentation

√ blocked paragraphs with regular left margin
  or
√ indented paragraphs with regular number of spaces indented on first line
√ same number of clear line spaces between paragraphs
√ same number of clear spaces after numbering or lettering of paragraphs (i.e. 1. 2. 3. or a) b) c) or roman numerals ranged to the right)
√ at least one clear space after longest roman numbering of paragraphs if ranged to the left, i.e.
                          (i)
                          (ii)
                          (iii)

Note:
You will receive one presentation fault for each *type* of inconsistency within a document.

PRAXITELES GROUP

A fictitious organisation for examination purposes only

PRAXITELES HOUSE · ADAM STREET · LONDON WC2N 6EZ
TELEPHONE 01 930 5115

Our ref   DER/TW

Your ref

(Date)

Please retype correctly

Mrs F J Lucas
"Highdene"
Wellingbourne Road
TELFORD
Shropshire   TS42 8OX

12 Fachter Road

Dear Mrs Lucas

Thank you for your (lettre). I note your (cmmments) regarding the (poosibility) of sending out a second Contract for the sale of the above property. Whilst the issuing of a second Contract is in (no way) "sharp practice" - provided all parties are informed of the fact that (anotrher) Contract is in (existnce) - it may have the effect of deterring interested parties from continuing with their pro proposed purchase. (Tehy) may consider that they will be (wasing) their time and money by competing for one specific property.

I have in fact now heard from the Solicitors acting for Mr Cox and Miss Adams. I enclose a copy of the draft Contract for your approval. Please read this document through (caerfully) and, provided that the details are correct, sign where indicated with pencil crosses and return all three pages as soon as possible.

(Hours) sincerely

D E (reddings)

Task 27

> JA Jones Esq
> 28 Church Street
> BENTOWN Wiltshire BV61 OCD
>
> Dr. Mr J_____
>
> The clauses (in our agreement) th. have been reworded are as follows:
>
> a. Clause 17: There wl. be no further meetings during the period of the same yr.
>
> b. Clause 28: Each representative wl. have one vote wh. may be cast in his/her absence by an authorised person.
>
> c. Clause 40: ~~Do not The words appear~~ The wording of such certificates to be agreed.
>
> We are arranging for full copying to be completed this week.
>
> Yrs. scly.

(f) ALTERNATIVE SPELLINGS

If a draft contains the word 'organise', for example, and you usually spell it as 'organize', you should not expect to have to change your habit unless you are working in an office that has a particular rule or requirement not to use certain spellings. This applies *only* to words for which alternative spellings can be found in an English dictionary.

IN THE EXAM

No words will be deliberately spelt two ways in order to test your spelling or any other skills. Therefore, you may copy what is written in the exam paper, *or* you may use your normal spelling if that is different.

WHAT THE EXAMINER WILL LOOK FOR

Presentation

! inconsistent change of spelling of the same word within a task

Part Two *Practice material (2)*

Complete Tasks 45 – 48. Read your work carefully. If necessary, make corrections. Then pass it to your checker. When you get it back, fill in your progress report (see page 52).

Task 45

Letter to Mr A H Fielding
139 Viewpoint
FENTON
Middlesex
FT1 6AS

carbon copy & envelope please

Dear Mr F——
Thank you for yr. remittance of £90.28 to open an a/c. with this Group. Your A/c. No will be 61166255 and interest wl. accrue with immed. effect. I have pleasure in enclosing your pass book wl. shd. be kept carefully as it is the only official receipt recognised by the Group. // I am arranging for a copy of the Group's latest annual a/cs. (as required by law) to be sent to you. // I wd. like to welcome you to the Group & assure you of the personal service of my staff & myself.
Yrs. scly.

General Manager.

(g) FRACTIONS

Fractions supplied on keyboards vary among typewriters. When you need to type fractions that do not occur on your keyboard, you can make them by combining what is available. For example,

$$\frac{3}{16} \qquad or \qquad 3/16$$

IN THE EXAM

Few fractions will appear in the exam paper.

The syllabus requires you to be consistent in the way you type fractions that are not included on your keyboard. For instance, there could be three fractions in an exam task and only one of them may be found on your typewriter:

We required a 3/16 inch spanner. It was supplied with the 1/3 inch steel rod about 1½ hours later.

You are most likely to have a key for '½', which you should use to type '1½ hours later'. If you do have keys for the other fractions, then of course you should use them. However, if you have to type two of the fractions required, then do so in the same way. For example:

We required a 3/16 inch spanner. It was supplied with the
1/3 inch steel rod about 1½ hours later.

or

We required a $\frac{3}{16}$ inch spanner. It was supplied with the $\frac{1}{3}$
inch steel rod about 1½ hours later.

WHAT THE EXAMINER WILL LOOK FOR

Accuracy

! each inaccurate fraction will be counted as a word fault

Presentation

√ same style of typing if more than one of the fractions is not a keyboard character

Chapter C3 on consistency looked at what line spacing you could choose if the task gave no instructions. This chapter covers instructions to you to use particular line spacing.

As a typist you will be expected to be able to vary the spacing within a document as instructed, and you will also find this a useful tool when typing correspondence, etc., for yourself. For instance, a change of line spacing can draw attention to sections of text, and if only large stationery is available a short draft will look more balanced if typed in double-line spacing.

There is, of course, nothing difficult about following this type of instruction so long as you know how to use the line-space regulator. However, if an instruction applies to only one section of the document you must *remember* to change the spacing for the rest of the task.

IN THE EXAM

Instructions regarding line spacing may be given to you:

(a) for the whole task. For example, 'Type in double-line spacing'. While following such an instruction you are safe in typing the sheet from beginning to end in double-line spacing, but you are not expected to discard any refinements you usually include in your work by the special uses of line spacing (see pages 69 – 70). For instance, if the instruction 'Type in double-line spacing' appeared in a letter, you would not be penalised for typing the inside address in single-line spacing. Equally, if the same instruction appeared within a table or other work with a main heading, you would not be penalised for leaving an extra line space between the end of the main heading and the rest of the document.

(b) for part of a task. For example:

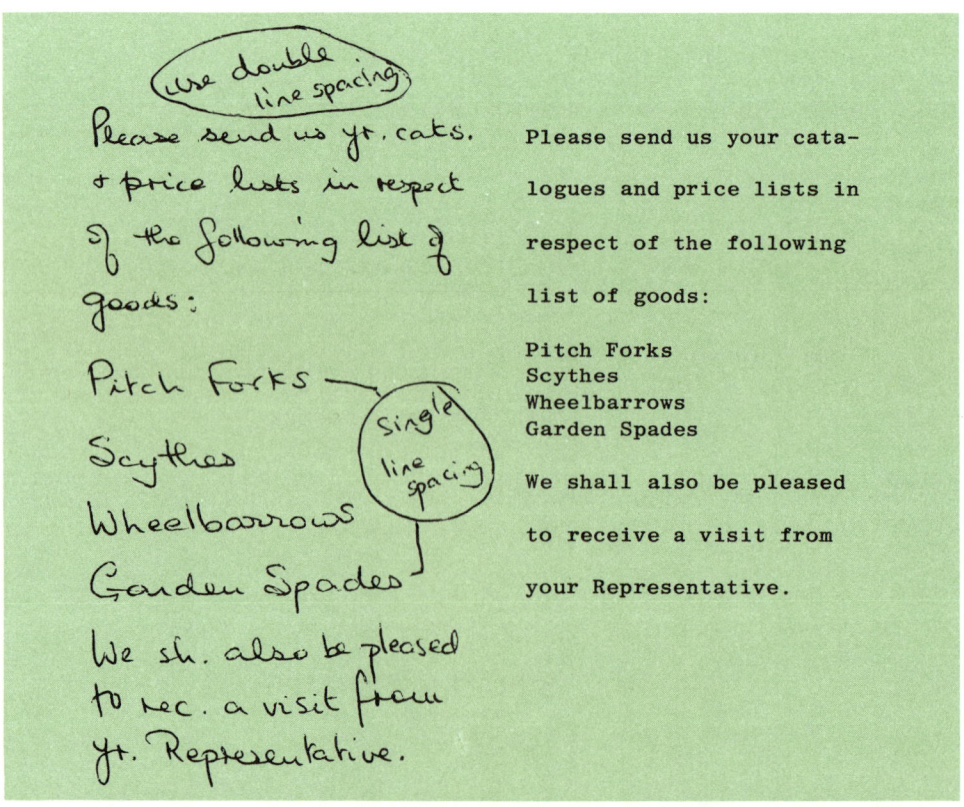

Task 28

COME AND JOIN OUR NEW CLUB

THERE ARE 1½ TIMES THE NUMBER OF FACILITIES

BUT THE FEE IS LESS THAN BEFORE

The premises will be open for 3¼ hours each day including Sundays.

People entitled to Membership:

Under 14   - Junior Section

14 - 21   - Young Seniors

22 - 30   - Seniors

Over 30   - Establishment Members

(h) LINE SPACING

This section will help you to decide what line spacing to choose when you have been given no instructions to use or to leave particular spacing between lines.

In business, it seems to be accepted practice that particular line spacing is used for some purposes. For instance, in letters *single-line spacing* is usually used when typing:

(a) inside address

(b) first two lines of the closing:

```
Yours faithfully
PRAXITELES GROUP
```

(c) last two lines of the closing:

```
J A Harkness
Sales Director
```

In notices, advertisement drafts or tables it is usual to use *double-line spacing* when typing main headings, for example:

```
TWO SUMMER TIMETABLES FOR

BRITISH RAIL AND ROAD TRANSPORT
```

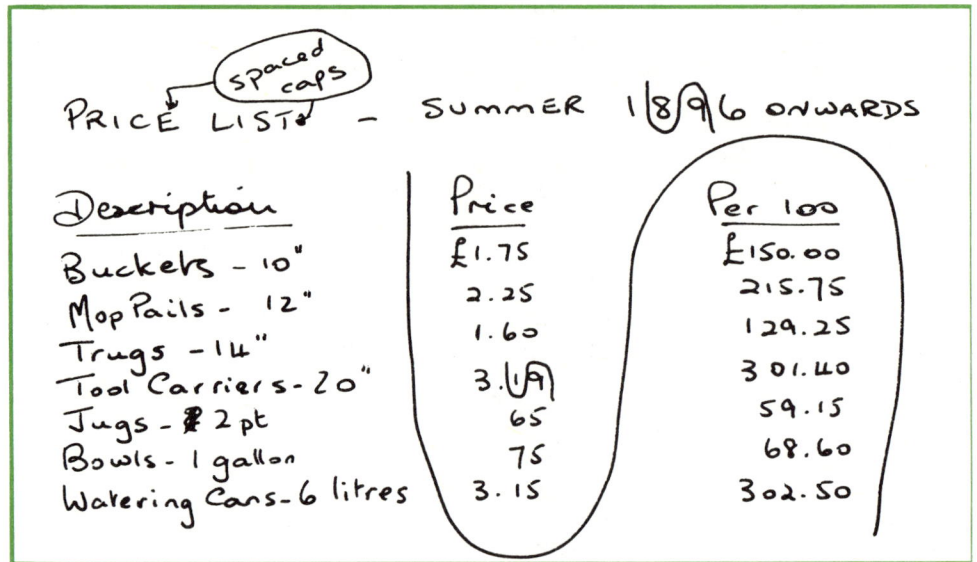

PRICE LIST (spaced caps) - SUMMER 1/8/96 ONWARDS

Description	Price	Per 100
Buckets - 10"	£1.75	£150.00
Mop Pails - 12"	2.25	215.75
Trugs - 14"	1.60	129.25
Tool Carriers - 20"	3.19	301.40
Jugs - 2 pt	65	59.15
Bowls - 1 gallon	75	68.60
Watering Cans - 6 litres	3.15	302.50

Task 44

(Memo)

To Customer Complaints   From Sales. A-M Area's

Unanswered Queries

In reply to your memo of yesterday, the 6/queries referred to in our report for last month are:-

Customer	Query	Letter date
PLD	Delivery	10.2.86
Verity's	Price	14.1.86
Lamberts	Delivery	10.1.86
Fenwicks	Order details	10.1.86
Mastersons	Damage	Phone - 23.2.86
Martin & Phelps	Colour	Letter - 24.2.86
		Phone - 16.3.86
		1.4.86
		13.4.86

We trust you will now be able to reply satisfactorily to these customers.

You may have noticed other instances when the same line spacing seems to be used by most people; and you may have developed your own preferences in the use of an extra line space to separate, say, the main heading from the rest of a document or the different sections of a paper.

IN THE EXAM

Unless you are given instructions to use particular line spacing, or to leave a given number of line spaces between items, you will not be penalised for your line spacing (unless it is irregular, for example, slipping from double to single within paragraphs).

Remember

If you are given an instruction to use the smaller paper, A5, then before choosing to use double-line spacing you will need to check that the material will still fit on the paper.

WHAT THE EXAMINER WILL LOOK FOR
Presentation

√ regular line spacing within paragraphs
√ same number of lines left clear between paragraphs
√ at least one clear line space before and after headings and separate items in a letter, for example, reference, date

C3 *Practice material*

Task 29

YOUNG WORKER REQUIRES WORK

ANY OFFICE WORK CONSIDERED

Wolverhampton area. Prepared for homework or travel to ~~this~~ co. office. Own typewriter. Good at text processing and simple numerical functions.

Tel. (0902)-1284867

presentation, the syllabus allows you to do so – but you need to be able to produce work centred accurately and consistently within the time allowed.

C6 *Practice material*

Task 42

J K Petch Ltd
21 Marlowe Road
Packington BURNLEY BY16 12 TI

Dr. Suis

Our letter of 21 March asked for yr. confirmation that yr. electric motor CM3 wd. be compatible w. our DK1/2 wh. uses yr. armature AM142. Yr. reply dated 1 April does not in fits fact give us the information we require. To clarify our problem we set out below the units concerned:

Motor	Armature	Field Core
DK 1/2		
DK 1	AM142	43.516
DK 2	AM142A	43.620
	AM140	40.982

Perhaps you wd. now be good enough to contact us again.

Yours ffly.

B EGAR
Factory Supplies

Ms Joan Pellingham
14 Avery Road
Eldington
Wishaw   Warwickshire   WW10 8TD

Dr. Joan

We sh. be more than happy to arrange for yr. return to work next month by offering you travel facilities & reduced hours. [The terms & conditions th. apply under yr. contract wl. be amended as you suggest & we quote from the new document:

"Hours of work: 10 am to 4 pm.

Travel to & from co. premises to be provided by the co. in the form of taxi, private car or co. van."

Yours sdy.
for PRAXITELES GROUP

J, Day
Personnel Office

(i) LEADER DOTS

If work is arranged in columns it is sometimes difficult for a reader to see which items are linked, particularly if there is a wide space between the columns.

A line of dots helps to lead the eye. For example:

Model	Price
Ford Escort	£4,600
Ford Granada de luxe	10,800
Vauxhall Cavalier Estate Car	7,295
Audi 2000	4,800

Note:
If you can end the leader dots at the same point, this is a refinement that you may feel adds to the appearance of your work.

Every word has to have a space after it, so do not start leader dots without leaving a space after the word in the first column.

If you wish to use a style of grouping leader dots in 'batches' of, say, two, three or four, do make sure that they are consistent. The batches must have the same number of dots, be aligned underneath each other, and have the same number of spaces between them.

(b) *Letters*

```
                Ref. AWC/RN              6 March 1986


                Messrs A & W Benton Ltd
                22 Church Lane
                FERRYBUN   Hants    FH17 3EX


                Dear Sirs


                     Your Order A621


                We shall supply these goods in 2
                weeks' time as requested.


                     Yours faithfully
                     DEMIJOHN COMPANY



                     Sales Department
```

(c) *Centring material typed in columns*

```
                     BERRICOMBE COATS

                Models available in August

            Cat No.      Colour         Quantity

            A6           Blue             400
            D6284        Green             10
            G21          Ash Blue         650
```

The above example shows equal left and right margins, with two main headings centred over the table. A more advanced style would involve centring the longest line in each of the columns under the column heading.

If you are already working as a typist and usually centre headings, tables, etc., then you should not change your method of presentation for the purpose of the exam. The syllabus allows you to choose the method with which you are more familiar.

IN THE EXAM

All of the work in the Stage I exam is acceptable in blocked style. There is no instruction, or need, to centre work either horizontally or vertically.

Remember

If you have learnt and are in the habit of using the centred style of

Remember

Each 'batch' of leader dots will be classed as a word – so leave a space after your last leader dot.

WHAT THE EXAMINER WILL LOOK FOR

Accuracy

! no space after words (including 'batches' of leader dots)
! inaccurate keyboarding (all the leaders must be dots)

Presentation

√ continuous line of leader dots
or
√ batches grouped and aligned consistently

C3 *Practice material*

Task 31

VENUES FOR REGIONAL STAFF CONTEST

<u>17 September 1986</u>

Birmingham . . . . - . . . - - - Grand Hotel
Tamworth . . . . - . . . . . - - .. Castle Hotel
Wolverhampton . . . . . - - - - - - The Victoria
Derby - - . The Wentworth
Stafford . . . . Paling's

Note that column 1 starts at the left margin and that each line in columns 2 and 3 is typed from the starting point for its own column (like its own left margin). This method of typing work in columns is also called 'ranged to the left' (see also page 74).

You will see that no instructions are needed on blocked style for *notices and letters*, since the typist merely sets the left margin at, say, 25 mm (1 in.) and starts each line there. A right margin should be set to make sure that typing does not reach or pass the edge of the paper.

For typing *material in columns*, the main headings can be presented in the same way, that is, setting the left margin at, say, 25 mm (1 in.). The first column is also typed from this left margin. To find the point at which to start the second and third columns, you will need to leave room for the longest line in the first column plus spaces between the columns (e.g. five) and set a tabulator stop for the second column. Tap the space bar to leave room for the longest line in the second column plus the same number of spaces as you had between the first and second columns and set a tabulator stop for the third column.

Blocked style is almost invariably acceptable in offices for tables with columns and notices, etc. A few offices have a house style in which, for instance, letters have the date typed on the right-hand side (see page 12); and in which paragraphs in letters and memoranda are 'indented' (see pages 65 – 6).

CENTRED

This means work is placed so that left and right margins are equal (horizontal centring). Occasionally, office work may require vertical centring (equal margins at top and bottom of the paper).
This applies to:

(a) *Notices*

STAFF   DANCE

to be held

at

PENDINGSHALL WORKS CANTEEN

on

Saturday 5 November

Contents

	Page No
Flowering	
Trees - ..	26
Fruiting Shrubs and Trees	7
Flowering Shrubs	20
Shrubs for Foliage	32
Flowers	1
Annexes	
Illustrations:	
Crab Apple . . . . . - - - - - - - ..	38
Roses	42-44
~~Potentilla . . . . . .~~	~~33~~
Holly	45
History of the Organisation	51

(j) MATERIAL IN COLUMNS

Presenting material in columns can be a useful way of communicating complicated information quickly and clearly.

In an office columns may appear as part of letters, memos and reports as well as in separate tables and accounts.

If you can use these machine parts:

- margin set,
- tabulator set and clear,
- tabulation key/bar,
- space bar

then you can present material in columns to the level required for general and routine work.

For tables (not as part of other documents) you could adopt a standard procedure, such as:

(a) leave 25 mm (1 in.) clear at the top of the paper;

(b) leave 25 mm (1 in.) left margin;

(c) use capitals or other form of emphasis indicated for main headings;

(d) where appropriate, type main headings in double-line spacing (and if you wish, you could add an extra line space after the end of the main heading);

(e) type column headings as indicated in the draft (usually with an initial capital letter and underlined);

(f) leave enough space between headings for the longest line in each of the columns (see also page 85);

(g) set a tabulator stop at the first letter of each column heading;

BLOCKED

This style means that each line starts at a left margin of, say, 25 mm (1 in.).

This applies to :

(a) *Notices*

```
S T A F F   D A N C E

to be held

at

PENDINGSHALL WORKS CANTEEN

on

Saturday 5 November
```

(b) *Letters*

```
Ref. AWC/RN

6 March 1986

Messrs A & W Benton Ltd
22 Church Lane
FERRYBUN  Hants    FH17 3EX

Dear Sirs

Your Order A621

We shall supply these goods in 2 weeks'
time as requested.

Yours faithfully
DEMIJOHN COMPANY


Sales Department
```

(c) *Material typed in columns*

```
BERRICOMBE COATS

Models available in August

Cat No.      Colour       Quantity

A6           Blue         400
D6284        Green        10
G21          Ash Blue     650
```

(h) leave a clear line space after column headings;
(i) type the columns in either double- or single-line spacing according to
    (i) instructions, *or*
    (ii) number of items and size of paper.

If numbers are included, they may be blocked – 'ranged to the left':

7061	and	£106.27
500		10.91
10		11.41
294		1.60
3		400.10

or 'ranged to the right':

7061	and	£106.27
500		10.91
10		11.41
294		1.60
3		400.10

When columns need to be totalled you will see it is preferable, and easier to check the addition, if the figures are ranged to the right.

When typing totals you also need to be consistent, and it is a good idea to adopt and memorise a simple routine, such as, 'underscore, turn up twice, type total, underscore' and use it consistently:

£26 824.50
156.14
1 720.75
1 300.61
£30 002.00

If you wish to use a different or more complicated method of typing totals, make sure you can remember your routine so that all your totals are presented in the same way.

IN THE EXAM

You will be required to type a three-column table with single-line column headings.

Remember

All work in the exam is acceptable in blocked format. If you choose to use centred style make sure you have equal margins either side of main headings; and if you centre column items under column headings (and vice versa), you must do so accurately.

(b) follow the draft:

```
OUR NEW CENTRE       OUR   NEW   CENTRE
is                   is
NOW OPEN!            NOW   OPEN!
LOW PRICES           LOW PRICES
Large Car Park       Large Car Park
```

Remember

You may centre lines if you wish, but it will take you more time than using blocked style, and it is not necessary even if the draft has lines which seem to be centred.

WHAT THE EXAMINER WILL LOOK FOR

Accuracy

! capitals added by you, not shown or requested on the draft
! capitals not typed, although appearing in the draft

Presentation

√ all instructions followed appropriately
√ consistent spacing between letters and/or words in capitals

You are not *required* to centre work horizontally (that is, with equal left and right margins) or vertically (that is, with equal top and bottom margins).

You must leave at least one clear space between columns (that is, after the longest line in each column).

WHAT THE EXAMINER WILL LOOK FOR

Accuracy

! each word not 100 per cent accurate – numbers (each group of figures) count as one word

Presentation

√ blocked style *or* centred style – consistently and accurately used
√ columns (of figures or words) ranged to the left (blocked) *or* columns (of figures) ranged to the right (tens under tens and so on)
√ totals with underlining and spacing the same each time

C3 *Practice material*

Tasks 33 – 36 ask you to type three-column tables with single-line headings.

Task 33

The Most Profitable and Successful Store

IN THE WORLD

CHARTER FLIGHTS FOR THE SALE ARRANGED FROM:-

USA	Canada	Paris
Monday	Monday	Tuesday
Wednesday	Tuesday	Friday
Saturday		Saturday

Task 34

BROADCASTING TOPICS - Week 28

Local	Regional	National
College Enrolment	Cats	Arts Council
Needlework Exhibition	Horse Show	National Opera Co.
	Politics Today	Libraries
Athletics Meeting	Home Crafts	Cookery

S P A C E D   C A P I T A L S

When typing spaced capitals you need to remember the space after each letter, and to leave three (or at the very least two) spaces between the words so that it is easy to see where each word ends.

CLOSED CAPITALS

When typing words in capital letters some people prefer to leave two spaces between the words.

Use the shift lock when typing in capitals, so as to get the best alignment.

Initial Capital Letters

These may be used on their own to give emphasis to a series of words, or combined with underlining.

Underlining

This is often referred to as 'underscoring'. It may be used on its own or combined with capitals in any of the three ways shown above.

Use the shift lock for underlining so as to get straight lines.

All of the above techniques can be used on any typewriter. Some electronic machines provide additional ways of emphasising, for example, typing words in bold type or in relief (white on black instead of black on white – the ribbon ink surrounding the letter outline).

IN THE EXAM

You need to understand how capitals and underlining can be used for emphasis so that you will be able (a) to follow any special instructions given on the use of capital letters and underlining and (b) to copy how the draft is written. For example:

(a) follow the instructions:

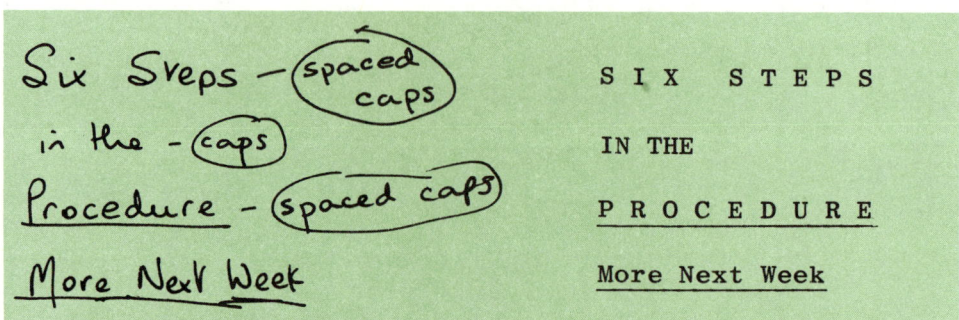

THE BUSINESS PAYS THE WAGES

The ratio of turnover to costs

Department	Turnover £m	Costs £m
Administration	–	14.0
Leather Goods	2.$5	0.5
Ladies Wear	6.0	1.0
Mens Wear	3.0	0.5
Footwear	3.5	1.5
Household Linens	5.0	2.0
Furniture	9.0	4.0
Jewellery	1.0	0.5

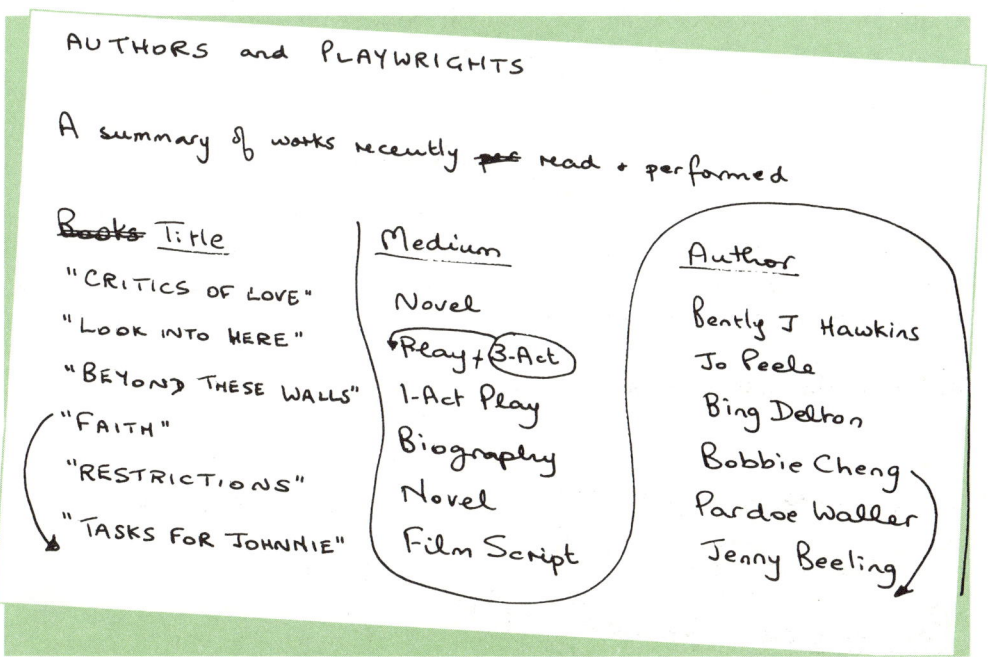

AUTHORS and PLAYWRIGHTS

A summary of works recently ~~per~~ read + performed

~~Books~~ Title	Medium	Author
"CRITICS OF LOVE"	Novel	Bently J Hawkins
"LOOK INTO HERE"	Play + 3-Act	Jo Peele
"BEYOND THESE WALLS"	1-Act Play	Bing Delton
"FAITH"	Biography	Bobbie Cheng
"RESTRICTIONS"	Novel	Pardoe Waller
"TASKS FOR JOHNNIE"	Film Script	Jenny Beeling

WHAT THE EXAMINER WILL LOOK FOR
Presentation

√ exact number of spaces from left-hand margin, as instructed
√ every line included in the inset, as indicated
√ return to main margin after insetting work
√ at least one clear line space before and one clear line space after the inset portion

C4 *Practice material*

Task 41

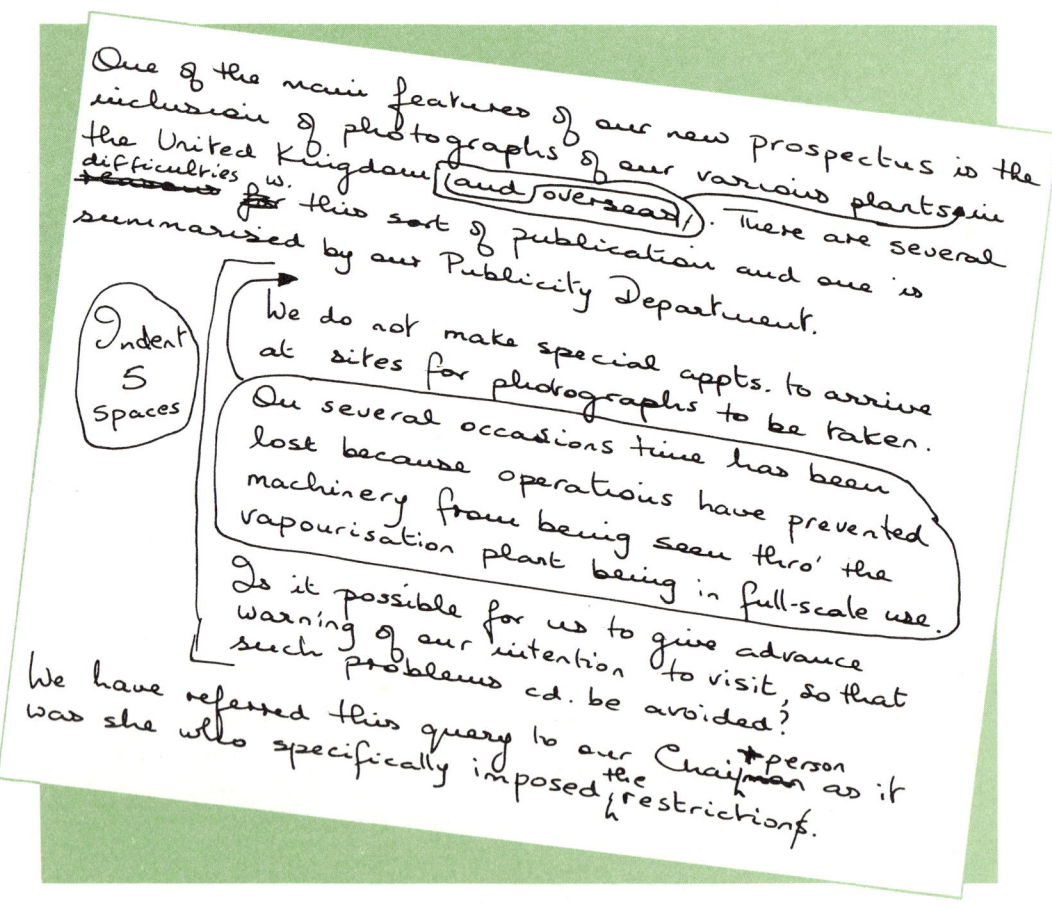

Complete Tasks 37 – 40. Read your work carefully. If necessary, make corrections. Then pass it to your checker. When you get it back, fill in your progress report (see page 52).

Task 37

Fellows & Jolley Ltd
22 Derry Lane
FECKENHAM   Warwickshire
FW491 6TA

(circled note: Take a carbon copy & type envelope)

For the attention of Mr. John Jolley

Dr. Sirs

This is to confirm the arrangements for yr. journey to Brussels next week.

Your Flight No is BA421 due to depart from Birmingham International Airport at 1206 hrs on Tuesday. You shd. arrive in time to check in at the Midlands Airways desk no later than 1115 hrs.

Your return flight has been booked for Thursday, Flight BA422, 1415 hrs from Brussels, for which you should check in no later than 1315 hrs at the British Airways desk.

As requested, we have pleasure in enclosing a timetable for 31.5.86 – 30.4.87.

Yours scly.
PRAXITELES TRAVEL SERVICES

This is a technique often used in business documents to call attention to certain lines, such as an extract from another document or a list of numbered items. For example:

> You will see that these few lines stand out from the rest of the page because they have been inset from the left margin. When insetting is combined with a change of line spacing, even greater emphasis is given to that part of the work, so that the reader notices it straight away.

It is not difficult to inset work – just move to the right of the margin either by moving the left-hand margin-set or by using the tabulator. However, it is *easy to forget to:*

- use the tabulator on every line (if you do not re-set the left margin);
or
- re-set the margin again to that used for the main text after you have typed the inset portion.

It is well worth while practising a procedure for insetting – and one of the steps should be to make a pencil mark on the draft task to remind yourself at the point when you should return to the main left-hand margin.

IN THE EXAM

The lines to be inset will be clearly marked, and you will be told how much space to inset from the left margin. For example:

> Our catalogue is being reproduced at present and includes the following paragraph:
>
> The manufacturers are not able to guarantee every delivery will be in the same colour.
>
> Inset 5 spaces
>
> We trust this will make clear the position on...

```
Our catalogue is being reproduced at present and includes
the following paragraph:

     The manufacturers are not able to guarantee every
     delivery will be in the same colour.

We trust this will make clear the position on ...
```

Task 38

Memo to Brussels Desk   from ↑ General Bookings

Attached is a copy of letter to Mr John Talley of F—— + J—— Ltd, Feckenham. This is to remind you that Mr J—— is a regular traveller + customer + th. his reservation includes an excess baggage allowance of 10 kilos.

He is also allowed a 2½% discount on all charges except airport taxes.

We have ~~sent~~ debited him on Invoice 38/BA/6218 dated today.   You shd. charge us thro' the localisation a/c. in the normal way.

Task 39

Monthly Returns

E U R O P E A N   S A L E S

JUNE-DECEMBER 1985

	Brussels	Frankfurt
First Class	42	38
Economy	159	212
Apex	206	48
Business	88	73
Children	14	6
30-day	0	2
Excess Baggage	1	0

To: Personnel Officer

(Use Plain A4 paper)

US## Operations

We have agreed to ~~appt.~~ engage a Projects Manager ~~to start~~ for our expansion programme & I sh. be glad if you wl. arrange to discuss ~~with~~ this appt. w. me as soon as possible.

The main duties & responsibility wl. be to oversee the expansion of our bus. in the US## although there is little indication at present of

(:) ~~the~~ the extent of (how long) the programme and it is likely to take

⊘ (ii) how soon the scheme will be operational

I have other queries:

a) Is there anyone already in our co. in UK who deserves to be considered?

b) If not, is there a US-based employee we shd. consider?

c) Shd. it be necy. to ~~advertise~~ recruit from outside, where do you consider it best to place adverts.?

I wd. like to use a UK-based employee if possible because of the re-deployment aspect. It wd. be a pity to erode ⊘ ~~the~~ benefits to be gained thro' creating new opps. for UK staff ~~by~~ difficulties wh. cd. be avoided, eg the appt. of someone without the exp. to make the workers' transition period as smooth as possible.

Perhaps you wl. have some ideas on this.

T. Bolan

(Leave room for signature)

RSA
STATIONERY PAD

In order to help you prepare for the RSA Typewriting Skills Stage I exam, thirty-one of the tasks in this book require the use of special RSA stationery, the sort that you will meet in the exam. On the next thirty-one pages, you will find all the blank stationery that you need to complete these tasks. The stationery includes fifteen Praxiteles Group letterheads (this is the RSA's fictional organisation for exam purposes), nine memos and seven forms to be filled in with information given in the relevant tasks.

The stationery is the copyright of the RSA and must not be photocopied. Stationery pads containing ten replacement sets of stationery (that is, enough for ten students) can be purchased direct from Heinemann Educational Books, Freepost EM17, The Windmill Press, Tadworth, Surrey KT20 6BR. Please write in with your order (no stamp required).

ISBN 0 435 451731 320pp per pad (enough for ten students) 297 × 210 £5.95 non-net

MEMORANDUM

From

Ref

To

Date

TRUSTON COMPREHENSIVE SCHOOL

PUPIL'S PART-TIME EMPLOYMENT

Name of Pupil ....

Name of Employer ....

Address   ....

              ....

              ....

Telephone No ....

Business   ....

Nature of
Employment   ....

HOURS OF EMPLOYMENT

Monday   to

Tuesday   to

Wednesday   to

Thursday   to

Friday   to

Saturday   to

Lunch
Period   to

Total Hours

Signature   ....
              * Manager/Supervisor/Tutor

Date   ....

* delete as appropriate

MEMORANDUM

From   Ref

To   Date

PRAXITELES INSURANCE GROUP

PRAXITELES HOUSE · ADAM STREET · LONDON WC2N 6EZ
TELEPHONE 01 930 5115

To

Date:

Policy Number:..

Insured: ....

Premium: ....

Effective Date: ....

Please refer to sections .... below.

1 ☐ We confirm that cover has now ceased and the time on risk charge is as shown above.

2 ☐ Amendments noted. No revised document(s) necessary. Premium adjustment is as shown above.

3 ☐ Amendments noted. Revised document(s) attached. Premium adjustment is as shown above.

4 ☐ Duplicate document(s) attached.

5 ☐ Policy cancelled. Return document is as shown above.

6 ☐ Please remit the premium shown above without delay.

7 ☐

MEMORANDUM

From   Ref

To   Date

CAR PARKING PERMITS

NAME: ....

DEPARTMENT CODE: ....

I do/do not drive to work. (Please delete as applicable)

REGULAR VEHICLE	Make and Model	....
	Registration No	....
	Colour	....
SECOND VEHICLE	Make and Model	....
	Registration No	....
	Colour	....
USUAL CAR PARK:		....

I confirm that the information given above is correct, and I
will inform you of any changes to these details.

SIGNED   ....

DATE   ....

MEMORANDUM

From   *Ref*

To   *Date*

BOOKING FORM

Please reserve .... places at ....

from .... to ....

or (2nd choice) .... places at ....

from .... to ....

Number of tents .... and/or* caravans ....

	No.	Days	Cost £	Names in full (Block letters please)
Adults				
Students				
12-16				
5-11				
2-4				
Under 2				
TOTAL				

I enclose cheque/Postal Order* to the value of £
being a deposit of £5 per person.

NAME

ADDRESS

TEL. No.

Date .... Signed ....

Send this form with your remittance to: PRAXITELES FOLK CAMPS,
PRAXITELES HOUSE, ADAM STREET, LONDON WC2N 6AJ

* Delete as applicable.

MEMORANDUM

From

To

Ref

Date

PRAXITELES GROUP

A fictitious organisation for examination purposes only

PRAXITELES HOUSE · ADAM STREET · LONDON WC2N 6EZ
TELEPHONE 01 930 5115

Our ref

Your ref

Date ....

_____

_____

_____

_____

Dear Patient

I have made an appointment for you to attend Dr _____

out-patient clinic on _____ at _____

for _____

You should go to the _____

If there are any problems with the appointment please phone the Appointments

Desk on Extension _____

Yours sincerely

MEMORANDUM

From   *Ref*

To   *Date*

MEMORANDUM

From   *Ref*

To   *Date*

THIS FORM – FOR USE IN WORKING TASK 6 – MUST BE INSERTED INSIDE THE COVER
OF YOUR ANSWER BOOK AT THE CONCLUSION OF THE EXAMINATION. IF BOTH SIDES
OF THIS FORM ARE USED ONE ATTEMPT MUST BE CANCELLED.

ORDER

ORDER NO.

VILLIERS ENGINEERING

25 GREEN STREET

LONDON NW4 6XL

TO

DATE

CODE NO.	QTY.	DESCRIPTION	UNIT PRICE £	PRICE £	p

TOTAL £

SIGNED

FOR EXPORT

MEMORANDUM

From   *Ref*

To   *Date*

MEMORANDUM

From   *Ref*

To   *Date*

S T U D I O   P R I N T S   L I M I T E D

67 The Broadway London WC1A 4RT   Telephone: 01-957 2438

ORDER FOR COLOUR PRINTS

NAME AND ADDRESS

PROOF NUMBER	SIZE	NUMBER REQUIRED
. . . .	. . . .	. . . .
. . . .	. . . .	. . . .
. . . .	. . . .	. . . .
. . . .	. . . .	. . . .
. . . .	. . . .	. . . .
. . . .	. . . .	. . . .

SIGNATURE . . . .

DATE . . . .

MEMORANDUM

From   *Ref*

To   *Date*

MEMORANDUM

From   *Ref*

To   *Date*

PRAXITELES GROUP

A fictitious organisation for examination purposes only

PRAXITELES HOUSE · ADAM STREET · LONDON WC2N 6EZ
TELEPHONE 01 930 5115

Our ref

Your ref

MEMORANDUM

From   *Ref*

To   *Date*

PRAXITELES GROUP

A fictitious organisation for examination purposes only

PRAXITELES HOUSE · ADAM STREET · LONDON WC2N 6EZ
TELEPHONE 01 930 5115

Our ref

Your ref

PRAXITELES GROUP

A fictitious organisation for examination purposes only

PRAXITELES HOUSE · ADAM STREET · LONDON WC2N 6EZ
TELEPHONE 01 930 5115

Our ref

Your ref

PRAXITELES GROUP

A fictitious organisation for examination purposes only

PRAXITELES HOUSE · ADAM STREET · LONDON WC2N 6EZ
TELEPHONE 01 930 5115

Our ref

Your ref

PRAXITELES GROUP

A fictitious organisation for examination purposes only

PRAXITELES HOUSE · ADAM STREET · LONDON WC2N 6EZ
TELEPHONE 01 930 5115

Our ref

Your ref

PRAXITELES HOUSE · ADAM STREET · LONDON WC2N 6EZ
TELEPHONE 01 930 5115

PRAXITELES GROUP

A fictitious organisation for examination purposes only

PRAXITELES HOUSE · ADAM STREET · LONDON WC2N 6EZ
TELEPHONE 01 930 5115

Our ref

Your ref

PRAXITELES GROUP

A fictitious organisation for examination purposes only

PRAXITELES HOUSE · ADAM STREET · LONDON WC2N 6EZ
TELEPHONE 01 930 5115

Our ref

Your ref

PRAXITELES GROUP

A fictitious organisation for examination purposes only

PRAXITELES HOUSE · ADAM STREET · LONDON WC2N 6EZ
TELEPHONE 01 930 5115

Our ref

Your ref

PRAXITELES GROUP

A fictitious organisation for examination purposes only

PRAXITELES HOUSE · ADAM STREET · LONDON WC2N 6EZ
TELEPHONE 01 930 5115

Our ref

Your ref

PRAXITELES GROUP

A fictitious organisation for examination purposes only

PRAXITELES HOUSE · ADAM STREET · LONDON WC2N 6EZ

TELEPHONE 01 930 5115

Our ref

Your ref

PRAXITELES GROUP

A fictitious organisation for examination purposes only

PRAXITELES HOUSE · ADAM STREET · LONDON WC2N 6EZ
TELEPHONE 01 930 5115

Our ref

Your ref

PRAXITELES GROUP

A fictitious organisation for examination purposes only

PRAXITELES HOUSE · ADAM STREET · LONDON WC2N 6EZ
TELEPHONE 01 930 5115

Our ref

Your ref

PRAXITELES GROUP

A fictitious organisation for examination purposes only

PRAXITELES HOUSE · ADAM STREET · LONDON WC2N 6EZ
TELEPHONE 01 930 5115

Our ref

Your ref

PRAXITELES GROUP

A fictitious organisation for examination purposes only

PRAXITELES HOUSE · ADAM STREET · LONDON WC2N 6EZ
TELEPHONE 01 930 5115

Our ref

Your ref

PRAXITELES GROUP

A fictitious organisation for examination purposes only

PRAXITELES HOUSE · ADAM STREET · LONDON WC2N 6EZ
TELEPHONE 01 930 5115

Our ref

Your ref